The 500 Hidden Secrets of

DUBLIN

INTRODUCTION

This travel guide is for those curious newcomers or the returning and/or adventurous visitors who want to find something new to tell others about. The 500 entries have been carefully selected after much list-making and deliberation.

The author, who has lived in Dublin all his life, selected some lesser known destinations off the beaten track that might intrigue and surprise. There will, of course, be some places in this book you may know already, like Dublin Castle or St Stephen's Green: they are known for a reason, and a must-visit. But there should be plenty of still undiscovered treasures as well, like the bar that's also a hardware store or the hidden lane off Dame Street that opens out into a colourful courtyard. Dublin is a rich tapestry of green spaces, trendy enclaves and comfortable corners. Hopefully within these pages there's a little something for everyone.

The findings in this guide are far beyond the author's personal favourites as he tried to accommodate the many walks of life that may visit Dublin. Hence the history buff, the foodie and the pub crawler are all catered for, with lists like '5 important places in the history of Dublin', '5 seafood restaurants not to miss' or 'The 5 best beer gardens'.

While Dublin cannot compete with Berlin and London when it comes to sheer size and scale, the author likes to think that in it's own charming way, Dublin has a certain magnetism and distinct character that can still prove very alluring for a multitude of reasons, which he touches upon within these pages. He hopes the book will show Dublin in a good light, a place of hospitality, of good atmosphere and of memorable moments.

HOW TO USE THIS BOOK?

This guide lists 500 things you need to know about Dublin in 100 different categories. Most of these are places to visit, with practical information to help you find your way. Others are bits of information that help you get to know the city and its habitants. The aim of this guide is to inspire, not to cover the city from A to Z.

The places listed in the guide are given an address, including the neighbourhood (for example St Stephen's Green & Grafton St or Temple Bar), and a number. The neighbourhood and number allow you to find the locations on the maps at the beginning of the book: first look for the map of the corresponding neighbourhood, then look for the right number. A word of caution however: these maps are not detailed enough to allow you to find specific locations in the city. You can obtain an excellent map from any tourist office or in most hotels. Or the addresses can be located on a smartphone.

Please also bear in mind that cities change all the time. The chef who hits a high note one day may be uninspiring on the day you happen to visit. The hotel ecstatically reviewed in this book might suddenly go downhill under a new manager. This is obviously a highly personal selection. You might not always agree with it. If you want to leave a comment, recommend a bar or reveal your favourite secret place, please visit the website *www.the500hiddensecrets.com* – you'll also find free tips and the latest news about the series there – or follow *@500hiddensecrets* on Instagram and leave a comment.

THE AUTHOR

Shane O'Reilly has lived in Dublin all his life. That's 34 years of memories and adventures around the city centre. During this time he rode out the recession and watched as his friends emigrated. While doing so he took a renewed interest in the Dublin he once knew. He watched it change and develop bringing with it artisan foods and craft beers, fashionable coffee bars, pop-up stalls and a donut revolution. Throughout it all, he always kept an eye out for those tiny slivers of sunshine. And if he were lucky enough to find himself in the city on one of those sunny days you could count on him making the most of it, drink in hand. When the sun's out, there's nowhere else quite like Dublin.

Shane wants to thank Dettie, Hadewijch, Marc and everyone else at Luster Publishers that helped with the book, the proofreading, the editing and the fact checking. He would like to thank Sam for the photos that brought the book to life. He would also like to thank Wan Yi Chen for accompanying him to all the coffee shops, bars, clothes shops and eateries. It was tough work, all in the name of research. Last but not least, Shane wants to thank everyone that gave him tips and suggestions. Whether he used them or not, they were all appreciated.

DUBLIN

overview

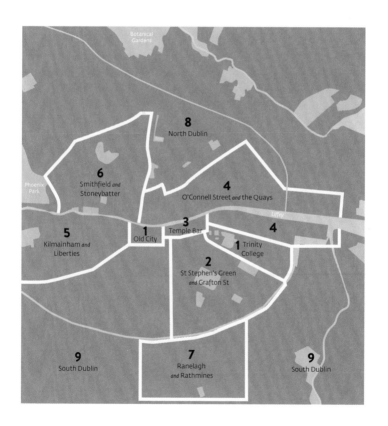

8 North Dublin

6 Smithfield *and* Stoneybatter

Phoenix Park

4 O'Connell Street *and* the Quays

Liffey

5 Kilmainham *and* Liberties

1 Old City

3 Temple Bar

4

1 Trinity College

2 St Stephen's Green *and* Grafton St

9 South Dublin

7 Ranelagh *and* Rathmines

9 South Dublin

Botanical Gardens

Map 1
TRINITY COLLEGE and
OLD CITY

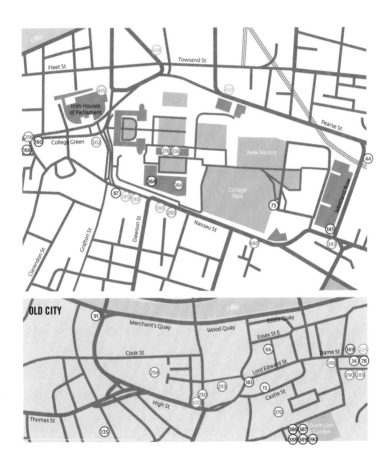

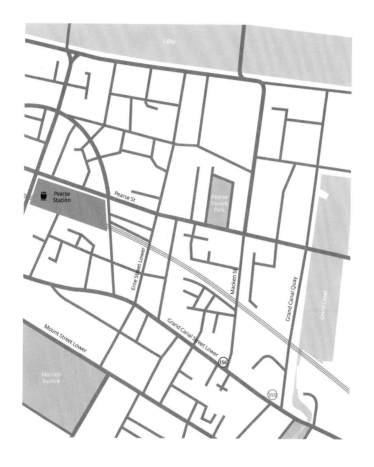

Map 2

ST. STEPHEN'S GREEN *and*
GRAFTON ST

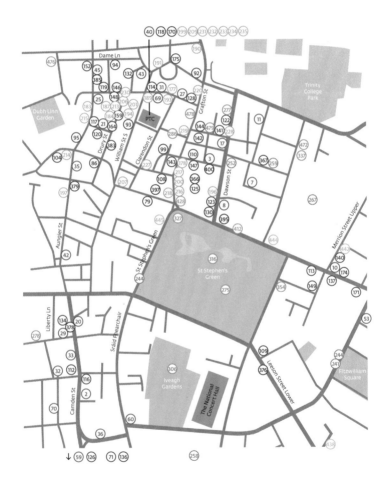

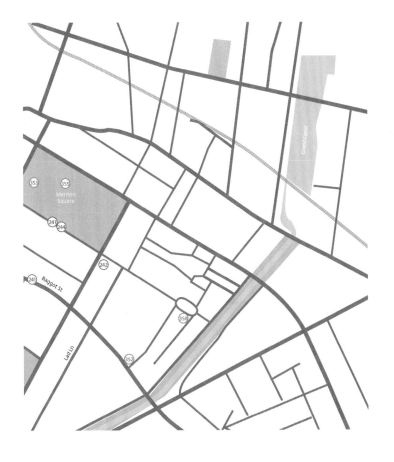

Map 3

TEMPLE BAR

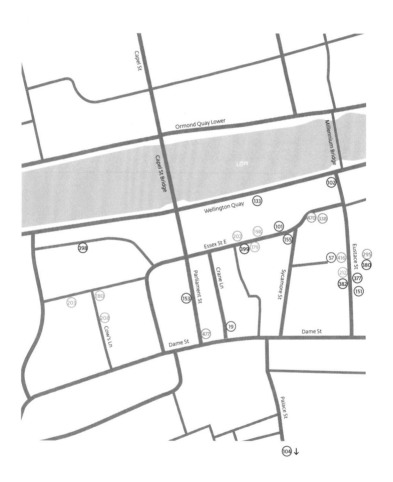

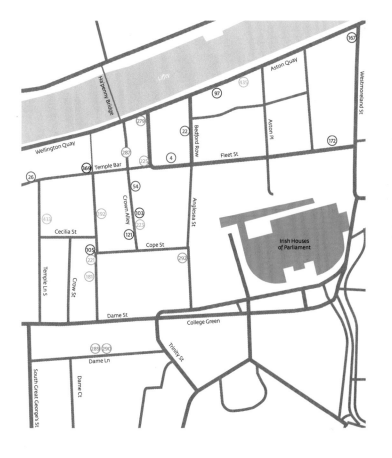

Map 4
O'CONNELL ST and
THE QUAYS

Map 5
KILMAINHAM *and* LIBERTIES

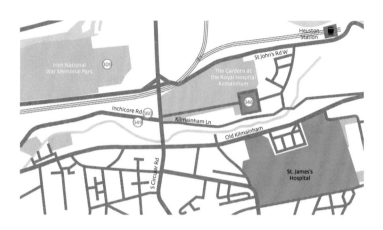

Map 6
SMITHFIELD *and* STONEYBATTER

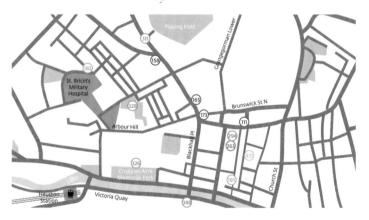

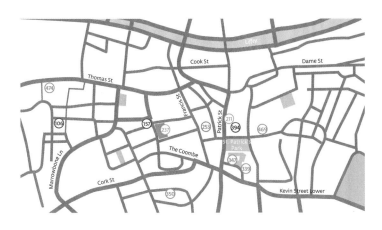

Map 7

RANELAGH *and* RATHMINES

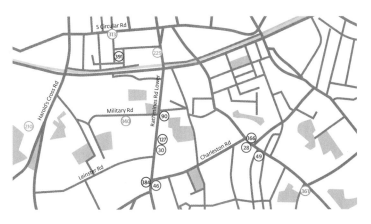

Map 8
NORTH DUBLIN

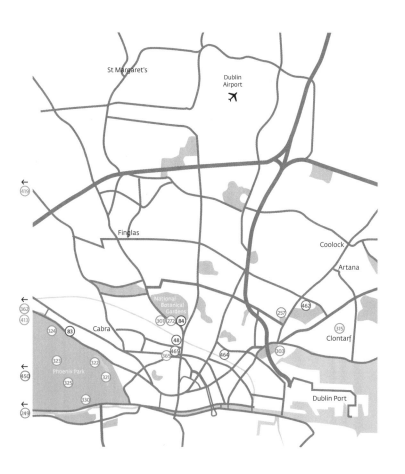

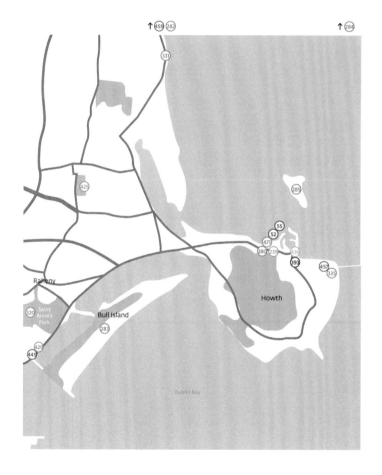

Map 9
SOUTH DUBLIN

333

Dublin Bay

317

12 204
6 236
Blackrock

5

82

427 430
Dún Laoghaire 222
238

332

51 344

Dalkey
312 58
85
47

363

281

Killiney
Hill
Park

273
Foxrock
↓ 460 421

334
Killiney

QUEEN OF TARTS

70 PLACES TO EAT OR BUY GOOD FOOD

---

5 of the best places for
IRISH
FOOD

---

1 **THE WINDING STAIR**
   40 Ormond Quay Lower
   O'Connell Street &
   the Quays ④
   +353 (0)1 872 7320
   www.winding-stair.com

Besides being a beautiful bookshop, The Winding Stair is also a restaurant of some renown. This is proper imaginative Irish cooking using only the best of locally sourced ingredients. The Winding Stair stands for a mix of home cooking and artisan style, with an extensive microbrewery beer and wine list.

2 **LISTONS FOOD STORE**
   25-26 Camden St Lower
   St Stephen's Green &
   Grafton St ②
   +353 (0)1 405 4779
   www.listonsfoodstore.ie

Listons is wall to wall with delicious containers, bottles and boxes. There are perfect presents for foodies and there are snacks for immediate consumption, either ways, it's difficult not to buy something once you step inside. Aside from wines, charcuterie and cheeses, there are also breads to be torn apart and oils for dipping.

3 SHERIDANS CHEESEMONGERS

11 Anna St South
St Stephen's Green &
Grafton St ②
+353 (0)1 679 3143
www.sheridans
cheesemongers.com

The pong when you walk in the door is like nothing else, thanks to a hundred cheeses calling out all at once – in thick slices, in wheels, on shelves and countertops, in all shades of oranges and yellows. Next to some of the best Irish and European cheeses around, there are also some wonderful meats, including delicious Gubbeen chorizo.

4 THE BOXTY HOUSE

20-21 Temple Bar
Temple Bar ③
+353 (0)1 677 2762
www.boxtyhouse.ie

Right bang in the heart of Temple Bar sits the very Irish Boxty. If you have ever wanted to sit down to genuine Irish cuisine, this is the place. Hot filling coddle? Three different stews and Irish breads? You name it. There's also plenty of salmon, crab cakes, steak, beef and lamb to keep you going.

5 AVOCA FOOD MARKET & SALT CAFE

11-A The Crescent,
Monkstown
South Dublin ⑨
+353 (0)1 202 0230
www.avoca.com/explore/
our-cafes/saltcafe-
monkstown

There are many Avocas but this one sits amongst a wonderful row of eateries in a nice spot in Monkstown. Avoca is a very popular producer of incredible foods, salads and sauces. This is a deli/cafe/restaurant and everything in it is humming with freshness. The smells are impossible to ignore and everything just looks irresistible.

5 great
CLASSY
restaurants

---

6 **HERON & GREY**
19-A Main St, Blackrock,
Blackrock Market
South Dublin ⑨
+353 (0)1 212 3676
www.heronandgrey.com

One of Dublin's hidden gems ... until it won a Michelin-star in October 2016. Don't be fooled by its cutesy, cosy location: this is adventurous no-nonsense eating. The two choices of menus are categorised under 'Land & Sea' or 'Field & Forest'. Book well in advance.

7 **ONE PICO**
5-6 Molesworth Court,
School House Lane
St Stephen's Green &
Grafton St ②
+353 (0)1 676 0300
www.onepico.com

One Pico offers beautiful food often made up of extraordinary combinations bursting with flavour, presented in a unique way, with an unusual twist. For example, how about: duck and foie gras infused with truffle, pumpkin risotto and mussels or sika deer with an assortment of freshly picked veg and fruit. Exquisite.

8 **THE GREENHOUSE**
Off St Stephen's Green,
Dawson St
St Stephen's Green &
Grafton St ②
+353 (0)1 676 7015
www.thegreenhouse
restaurant.ie

The Greenhouse is very contemporary fine dining. Chef Mickael Viljanen offers a four and a six-course set menu five nights a week and a five-course surprise tasting menu on Friday and Saturday nights only. This is very refined and delicate food handled expertly with an artist's eye for presentation.

9   **MULBERRY GARDEN**
     Mulberry Lane
     Donnybrook
     South Dublin ⑨
     +353 (0)1 269 3300
     www.newmulberry.
     restaurantboomerang.com

Hidden away down a lane in Donnybrook, Mulberry Garden is situated on the grounds of an old cottage. Fiercely proud of their heritage, everything they serve has been locally sourced: the quail, the prawns, the butternut squash, the John Dory and the lamb. From your table you can gaze out across a stunning courtyard and garden.

10   **PEARL BRASSERIE**
     20 Merrion St Upper
     St Stephen's Green &
     Grafton St ②
     +353 (0)1 661 3572
     www.pearl-brasserie.com/
     restaurant-dublin

An award winning restaurant deep in Georgian Dublin, Pearl Brasserie takes modern French cuisine to a whole other level. With its ever changing and hugely inventive menu and its cosy, stylish and romantic interior, it's the perfect venue for semi-private group functions or a quiet candlelit dinner for two.

6 HERON & GREY

The 5 best
ITALIAN
restaurants

---

11 **DUNNE AND CRESCENZI**
16 Frederick St South
St Stephen's Green &
Grafton St ②
+353 (0)1 677 3815
*www.dunneand
crescenzi.com*

What started as a small Italian *alimentari* for Eileen Dunne and Stefano Crescenzi blossomed into a stunning restaurant business with authenticity stamped all over it. The menu offers big traditional dishes with bold flavours and staff are on hand to help with wines.

12 **CIAMEI CAFE**
19-A Main St, Blackrock,
Blackrock Market
South Dublin ⑨
+353 (0)86 897 8418
*www.blackrockmarket.
com/ciamei-cafe*

Dublin's best kept secret. This tiny cafe and restaurant, tucked away at the end of the meandering Blackrock Market, is capable of turning out incredibly tasty dishes. You can sit indoors and chat with the friendly staff or outside on any number of scattered chairs while having a glass of wine.

13 WALLACE'S TAVERNA

**24 Ormond Quay Lower
O'Connell Street &
the Quays ⑤
+353 (0)1 873 0040
*www.wallacewinebars.ie***

Wallace's Taverna is situated at the gateway to the Italian Quarter. There is a lot of choice here between the antipasti, the pasta dishes and over 100 wines. But you should try one of the 25 varieties of stone oven pizzas freshly made with a proper thin base, dripping with cheeses and an array of toppings.

14 DA MIMMO

**148 North Strand Road
North Dublin ④
+353 (0)1 856 1714
*www.damimmo.ie***

This family-run eatery is small and has a very friendly feel to it and a very friendly staff. Size means nothing however; Da Mimmo serves a huge menu with around 30 types of pizza and much more. Don't forget to order some of their homemade dipping sauces.

15 BOTTEGA TOFFOLI

**34 Castle St
Trinity College &
Old City ①
+353 (0)1 633 4022**

With little internet presence and seating for only a handful of people, Bottega Toffoli has certainly kept its mystic vibe. With the kitchen, counters and tables all within arms reach, it is the epitome of charming. The food is always exceptional and the menu changes almost daily, with everything made to order. An experience.

5 delicious
BUDGET BITES

---

16 BROTHER'S DOSIRAK
  27 Capel St
  O'Connell Street &
  the Quays ④
  +353 (0)87 771 4278
  *www.jnbcatering
  services.com*

This Korean style lunch box canteen in the back of an Asian supermarket is as authentic as it gets. For 7 or 8 euros you can order a huge portion of rice, miso soup, your choice of meats and a variety of side dishes. It's an absolute bargain and a great hidden gem. You can order online and take out or eat in-house.

17 YUM THAI
  13 Duke St
  St Stephen's Green &
  Grafton St ②
  +353 (0)1 670 8975

This tiny Thai noodle bar is a fairly regular haunt for the nearby Trinity students who know good food at a good price when they see it. You can sit indoors or outside on the bench and eat from the carton with your chopsticks. All the Thai classics are on offer here for very reasonable prices.

18 BOOJUM

Millennium Walkway
O'Connell Street &
the Quays ④
+353 (0)1 872 9499
www.boojummex.com

The king of burritos in Dublin. And if they weren't already mouth-watering enough, Boojum have umpteen different bottles of hot sauces lying around to juice up the fire. Try a different one with each bite. You're looking at around 10 euros for a burrito and a bottle of beer to wash/cool it down.

19 SKINFLINT

19 Crane Lane
Temple Bar ③
+353 (0)1 670 9719
www.joburger.ie/skinflint

The name says it all: Skinflint is here for those looking for that cheaper option without sacrificing flavour. Pizzas, salads and meatballs comprise most of the dinner menu but the lunch menu is an absolute steal with the soup and sandwich combos ranging from 5 to 8 euros. Try the homemade lemonade.

20 LAS TAPAS DE LOLA

12 Wexford St
St Stephen's Green &
Grafton St ②
+353 (0)1 424 4100
www.lastapasdelola.com

This authentic and very popular tapas restaurant has two premises in Dublin city centre serving up deliciously addictive morsels, like *jamon iberico*, *patatas bravas* and *calamari* to die for. The menu is formidable and very affordable whether you're there for a snack, a lunch or a dinner.

The 5 most authentic
ASIAN EATERIES

---

21 **DUCK HONG KONG BBQ**
   15 Fade St
   St Stephen's Green &
   Grafton St ②
   +353 (0)1 671 8484
   www.duck.ie

This authentic Hong Kong BBQ cooks using a 'bullet oven', so called because of its shape. The resulting crispy duck is likely to be the most succulent in Dublin. Originally only frequented by Asians and a few Irish in the know, this has now became a popular haunt for those looking for an alternative to pricy restaurants.

22 **BANYI JAPANESE DINING**
   3-4 Bedford Row
   Temple Bar ③
   +353 (0)1 675 0669
   www.banyijapanese dining.com

It looks like the real thing and it cooks like it too. The interior is beautifully decorated, with the two rooms divided by traditional *shōji*. The plum sake and the ramen are a must, and the friendly staff is always on hand to guide you over the menu should you like to try something more adventurous.

23 **OLD TOWN CHINESE RESTAURANT**
   123 Capel St
   O'Connell Street &
   the Quays ④
   +353 (0)1 873 3570

This is Cantonese cuisine at its finest. Lots of flavour and spices here, steamed fish and deep frying, with sauces like hoisin, oyster, black bean, sweet and sour. Also delicious are the deep red and brown soups and noodle dishes with a lot of bold textures and taste.

24 AOBABA

46-A Capel St
O'Connell Street &
the Quays ④
+353 (0)1 878 8555

The extremely colourful Aobaba is hard to miss and inside it's just as bright. Skip the tables and take the tall stools by the large front window. It's perfect to people-watch while you sample genuine *bánh mì*, crunchy *bun cha*, summer rolls or *pho*, all washed down with bubble tea or a fruit drink.

25 GOOD WORLD RESTAURANT

18 Great George's St South
St Stephen's Green &
Grafton St ②
+353 (0)1 677 5373
www.goodworldchinese
restaurant.goldenpages.ie

Take a seat at one of the large round tables draped with white linen and order yourself a Chinese beer. Dissect the enormous menu and try the pillowy dim sum, the sensational pork congee and anything else you desire and watch it all arrive at once with sides and condiments. This is a wonderful traditional affair.

21 DUCK HONG KONG BBQ

5 must-try
BURGER
restaurants

---

26 BUNSEN

22 Essex St East
Temple Bar ③
+353 (0)1 559 9532
www.bunsen.ie

Up until very recently, it was difficult to pinpoint Dublin's greatest burger. And the jury is still out. But Bunsen is in the top 3 for sure. They keep it simple (there's no bacon and only two types of burger) and the simplicity has paid off. They now have four outlets of mouthwatering delight in Dublin.

27 WOWBURGER

AT: MARY'S BAR
(DOWNSTAIRS)
8 Wicklow St
St Stephen's Green &
Grafton St ②
+353 (0)1 670 8629
www.wowburger.ie

You can queue and order your pints with your meal, take a ticket while enjoying your beer and wait for your number to be called. The prices are better than anywhere else (around €10 for a proper burger and fries) and there are ten free toppings to choose from. Try the chilli fries and the Wowburger sauce. Incredible.

28 DILLINGER'S

47 Ranelagh Road
Ranelagh &
Rathmines ⑦
+353 (0)1 497 8010
www.dillingers.ie

Often called the best burger in Dublin, Dillinger's serves a mean juicy smoky cheeseburger with crispy paprika onions, pickles and a special sauce. And it's that tangy tomatoey sauce and the perfect fat patty that puts this burger over the top. The fries are nothing special but there is a huge portion of them. Perfect for a brunch, a dinner, anytime really.

29 BÓBÓS

22 Wexford St
St Stephen's Green &
Grafton St ②
+353 (0)1 400 5750
www.bobos.ie

No other joint in town has been as imaginative or as inventive as Bóbós when it comes to creating a special burger. The place is well known for its extensive menu featuring 18 different types of beef burger, 2 pork, 2 lamb, 2 chicken, 2 fish and 2 vegetarian. For serious taste, just try 'The Mexican'.

30 FARMER BROWNS

170 Rathmines Road
Lower
Ranelagh &
Rathmines ⑦
+353 (0)86 046 8837
www.farmerbrowns.ie

These are big fat dinner burgers we're talking about now. If you want a classic, go for the 'The Farmer Burger', a tasty combination of prime beef, cheddar, red pepper, red onion and tomato. If you want a stacked challenge, try the 'Massey Ferguson': two patties, cheddar, bacon, onion rings and a sumptuous cola bourbon BBQ sauce.

5 *wonderful restaurants for*
VEGETARIANS

---

31 **CORNUCOPIA**
19-20 Wicklow St
St Stephen's Green &
Grafton St ②
+353 (0)1 677 7583
www.cornucopia.ie

Cornucopia has been around since 1986 and feels like an Irish institution at this point. The place has an incredibly warm and welcoming atmosphere and is immediately relaxing. The size of portions is generous and the variety of soups, salads and mains has always been both adventurous and delicious.

32 **SOVA FOOD**
VEGAN BUTCHER
51 Pleasants St
St Stephen's Green &
Grafton St ②
+353 (0)85 727 7509

Finally away from the markets with a permanent residence Sova Food Vegan Butcher is a 100% plant-based vegan restaurant. Its range of extremely healthy options from juices to lunches and dinners has become very popular. Sova may even sway true carnivores with their beautifully ornate dishes.

33 **MCGUINNESS**
TRADITIONAL TAKE AWAY
84 Camden St Lower
St Stephen's Green &
Grafton St ②
+353 (0)86 823 0000

You can still buy the usual stuff here – burgers, fish and chips, kebabs – but there is also a healthier side to McGuinness in the form of their vegan menu: all meat options have replica vegan alternatives. There's even a vegan battered sausage.

34 UMI FALAFEL

13 Dame St
Trinity College &
Old City ①
+353 (0)1 670 6866
www.umifalafel.ie

You could try the mouth-watering falafels but you could also embrace the colourful menu packed with exotic flavours; the homemade red pepper hummus is incredible, and the same goes for the hummus sandwich and the grilled haloumi cheese sandwich. Or you can have the 'Falafel Your Way' with your own pick of toppings.

35 GOVINDA'S

4 Aungier St
St Stephen's Green &
Grafton St ②
+353 (0)1 475 0309
www.govindas.ie

Govinda's is a Hare Krishna-run vegetarian restaurant with two successful locations in Dublin city. A fusion of European and Indian flavours, you won't just find the usual fare of soups, vegetarian burgers and homemade breads and dips, but also a fine selection of desserts, drinks, lassi and a purifying Shipibo Amazon Tea.

34 UMI FALAFEL

5 places to go for the
ULTIMATE SANDWICH

---

36 DOUGHBOYS
2 Charlotte Way
St Stephen's Green &
Grafton St ②
+353 (0)1 402 2000
www.doughboys.ie

Doughboys has only been around for a couple of years but it's already at the forefront of the sandwich business. Sandwiches need to pack a punch and fill you up and there are a few here that fit the bill. For my money try the 'Porchetta' (on Thursdays and Fridays) and the 'Italian Sub' and the 'Club Dough' any other day.

37 JUNIORS
2 Bath Avenue
South Dublin ⑨
+353 (0)1 664 3648
www.juniors.ie

You can see them the minute you step inside around lunchtime; mountains of sandwiches piled high, with pieces of greenery and tomato slices peeping out from them. This New York style cafe and deli has all the classics, and will have you salivating as your senses go into overdrive. Try 'The Hero'.

38 147 DELI
147 Parnell St
North ④
+353 (0)1 872 8481

It's all about very affordable, good quality sandwiches stuffed with ingredients here at 147. The cheese steak and the sumac chicken wrap are two really interesting choices but the reuben with corned beef is the winner hands down. Keep your eye out for the weekly specials.

39 OXMANTOWN

16 Mary's Abbey
O'Connell Street &
the Quays ④
+353 (0)1 804 7030
www.oxmantown.com

A number of great little eateries have sprung up all over Dublin 7 in recent years and Oxmantown is certainly one to check out. There's a black pudding sandwich for breakfast, and a tasty ham and cheese sandwich for lunch. And how about spending 5,50 euros on 'The Ruby': a superb pastrami sandwich with sauerkraut on rye?

40 THE PEPPER POT

AT: POWERSCOURT CENTRE
South William St
St Stephen's Green &
Grafton St
+353 (0)1 707 1610
www.thepepperpot.ie

The Pepper Pot menu offers something slightly different from, well, every other sandwich shop. There are tarts, bagels and big wholesome salads created with a lot of imagination, like the one with panfried goat's cheese, Gubbeen chorizo and vine tomatoes. But then there's the roast pear, bacon and cheddar sandwich and suddenly nothing else matters.

The 5 best places for
DONUTS

---

41 **THE ROLLING DONUT**
34 Bachelors Walk
O'Connell Street &
the Quays ④
+353 (0)1 534 5085
www.therollingdonut.ie

What started as a tiny kiosk way back in 1978 has finally expanded into a proper store, which is no wonder considering the donut revolution that Dublin is experiencing. These are probably the biggest donuts in the city and they cost a bit more than other places, but the variety is impressive. Vegan donuts are also available.

42 **AUNGIER DANGER**
37 Aungier St
St Stephen's Green &
Grafton St ②
+353 (0)1 556 2021
www.aungierdanger.ie

At the start of the donut craze, Aungier Danger were the first to become very popular. Now they have two permanent locations. The oreo & marshmallow and the nutella donuts are two must eats. For something a little lighter, try the delicious coffee waffle.

43 **BOSTON DONUTS**
13 Trinity St
St Stephen's Green &
Grafton St ②
+353 (0)87 631 1143

This big, bright and spacious place in a lovely side street heading down towards Dame Street has a very American feel to it, with echoes of Dunkin' Donuts from decades ago. Maybe a little pricy but the wide choice and the special offers make up for it.

44 OFFBEAT DONUT CO.
AT: PEARSE ST STATION
Westland Row
Trinity College &
Old City ①
+353 (0)1 670 6164
www.offbeatdonuts.com

Along with its handy location right at the DART station behind Trinity College (and a second, newer location on George's Quay), Offbeat Donut Co. serves quite possibly the best donuts in the city. Expect an array of unique delights like the ferrero roche donut or the rich chocolate ganache, and two classics done extremely well: the red velvet and the cinnamon sugar donut.

45 KRÜST BAKERY
5-6 Great George's St
South
St Stephen's Green &
Grafton St ②
+353 (0)1 551 7622
www.krustbakery.ie

This is a bakery like any other, in that it makes typical bakery products. But there are very fine donuts as well, and also 'cronuts': a wonderfull mix of donut and croissant. Here they sit, iced over, with all those light fluffy layers just waiting for you.

44 OFFBEAT DONUT CO.

5 different eateries
OUTSIDE
the CITY CENTRE

---

46 TIPPENYAKI RESTAURANT
39 Castlewood Avenue
Ranelagh &
Rathmines ⑦
+353 (0)1 497 9463
www.tippenyaki.ie

Tippenyaki is a Japanese cooking technique in which a large griddle or hot plate is used to cook many different things all at once. This is usually done in full view of the customers, adding a bit of flair and exuberance to your dining experience. Book early to get front row seats.

47 GUINEA PIG
17 Railway Road, Dalkey
South Dublin ⑨
+353 (0)1 285 9055
*www.guineapig.
dalkey.info*

More than 60 years ago the Guinea Pig restaurant opened its doors in the centre of the heritage town of Dalkey, drooping with beautiful hanging baskets and potted plants. Its reputation for superlative dishes straight from the ocean has attracted, and still attracts, a plethora of celebrities. Book early and you can join them from 5.30 pm onwards..

48 BANG BANG

59-A Leinster St North, Phibsborough
North Dublin ⑧
+353 (0)86 857 6054

It's a deli. It's a cafe. It's a shop. It's all these things and more – a market and a greengrocer's, for example. Everything is freshly sourced and homemade. There's a brunch burger with renown, but also some incredible vegan options. Or try the sandwiches, or an iced coffee and Silverskin coffee.

49 TRIBECA

65 Ranelagh Road
Ranelagh &
Rathmines ⑦
+353 (0)1 497 4174
www.tribeca.ie

Ask anyone about TriBeCa, the restaurant in the middle of fashionable Ranelagh, and undoubtedly the chicken wings will be mentioned. These are delicous, of course, but there's a lot to love here: the extensive menu has something for everyone with generous portions and beers, wines and cocktails to wash it all down.

50 STOOP YOUR HEAD

19 Harbour Road
Townparks, Skerries
North Dublin
+353 (0)1 849 2085
www.stoopyourhead.ie

This fantastic family-run seafood restaurant in Skerries lies right on the waterfront. They don't take bookings, so come early or just wait at the bar and enjoy a drink before being seated. Try the crab claws or Dublin bay prawns in garlic butter.

5 SEAFOOD RESTAURANTS

not to miss

---

51 CAVISTONS RESTAURANT

58-59 Glasthule Road, Sandycove
South Dublin ⑨
+353 (0)1 280 9245
www.cavistons.com/restaurant

One half stunning delicatessen, one half famed restaurant, serving up delicious seafood straight from the ocean half a mile away. This is a legendary family-run place with almost 70 years of excellence. The staff are very friendly and full of knowledge if you're looking for the perfect wine to pair with your meal.

52 THE OAR HOUSE

8 West Pier, Howth
North Dublin ⑧
+353 (0)1 839 4568
www.oarhouse.ie

You can't get any fresher seafood than at The Oar House: it comes straight from the ocean to this restaurant on the pier. This is a great and reasonably priced restaurant with a very comprehensive seafood menu. Try the mussels. Also keep an eye out for the grey seals outside who love being fed.

53 MATT THE THRESHER

31-32 Pembroke St
St Stephen's Green &
Grafton St ②
+353 (0)1 676 2980
www.mattthethresher.ie

This multi-award winning seafood bar and grill serves up to five or six different kinds of fresh fish each day; they're written on the boards which change twice daily. There's something for everyone here but try the luxury fish pie or share the seafood platter for two – it's incredible.

54 KLAW

5-A Crown Alley
Temple Bar ③
+353 (0)1 549 3443
www.klaw.ie

It may be small, it may be narrow and it may be stuck in Temple Bar – not exactly seafood-Mecca – but Klaw certainly serves up some of the best crab shack-style dishes: Crab Mac'N'Cheese, for instance. There's shellfish galore, lobster rolls and even an Oyster Happy Hour (everyday from 5 to 6 pm).

55 AQUA

1 West Pier, Howth
North Dublin ⑧
+353 (0)1 832 0690
www.aqua.ie

Aqua serves some of the very best and freshest seafood around and makes for a memorable fine-dining experience. The prices reflect the restaurant's stature, but believe us: if you book a table, you won't be disappointed. And, nothing beats the view from this award-winning restaurant right at the end of the pier, overlooking the Irish Sea.

54 KLAW

5 pop-up
MARKETS &
STREET FOOD STALLS

---

56 **ZERO ZERO PIZZA**
Wednesday to Friday
Various locations
www.zerozeropizza.ie

Freshly made and wood fired, these authentic Neapolitan pizzas are the perfect lunchtime bite. A Zero Zero Pizza outlet will open soon at 21 Patrick Street in Dun Laoghaire, but in the meantime you can try the mobile vendor. They'll make your pizza from scratch with tender loving care, and you can watch as the magic unfolds.

57 **THE GALLIC KITCHEN**
Sat: Temple Bar Food
Market
Meeting House Square
Temple Bar ③
9 am - 5 pm
Sun: Farmleigh, White's
Road
North Dublin ⑧
10 am - 5 pm
www.gallickitchen.com

Who doesn't like delicatessen foods? Pies, tarts, pasties, quiches, sauces and jams... After twenty years in the business the Gallic Kitchen has it all. Fresh and handmade, these are the perfect ingredients for a sit-down meal, picnic snack or takeaway dinner, all at a reasonable price.

58 THE REAL OLIVE COMPANY

Friday: Irish Farmers Market, Leopardstown Racecourse
South Dublin ⑨
10.30 am - 3.30 pm
www.therealoliveco.com

This Mediterranean food company has been trading in Ireland for over twenty years. Their market stall is always resplendent with buckets and buckets of incredible smells and colours, endless Toon Bridge cheeses, all kinds of olives, sun dried tomatoes, herbs and pesto.

59 VEGINITY

AT: EATYARD
Richmond Place South
St Stephen's Green & Grafton St ②
www.veginity.com

Veginity is an award-winning plant-based street food business. Australian chef Mark Senn worked at Mildreds in London's Soho and Soul Mama in Melbourne and became a bit of a celebrity: he's a published author and has his own vegan cooking channel on Youtube. The food here is elegant but hardy, made with plenty of imagination.

60 FRANK'S GERMAN SAUSAGES

AT: HARCOURT FOOD MARKET STATION BUILDINGS
Upper Hatch St
St Stephen's Green & Grafton St ②
Tues & Thurs:
10 am – 4 pm
www.dublincitymarkets.
com/promos/franksger-
mansausages.html

Why would anyone bother with regular sausages when there are endless beautiful *bratwursts* being barbequed nearby? Frank's are the real deal, with a real German cook behind the grill. If you don't like wurst, try any of the other finger food options and, if you're very lucky, the grilled salmon, that's sometimes on offer.

5 sandwich
C R I S P S *you should try*

---

61 TAYTO

These are the standard Irish crisps. They are so famous that they have travelled to the other side of the world and they have their own mascot (Mr. Tayto). There's even a Tayto theme park in Ashbourne, Co. Meath! Cheese and Onion may be their bestselling flavour, but all their flavours taste fantastic in any type of sandwich or roll.

62 KING

These are the packets of crisps you are most likely to find in pubs, usually the kettle or gold standard version. They are processed in batches, which somehow gives them more body and a bigger crunch. A close second to Tayto and more proof that Irish potatoes produce the best crisps worldwide.

63 HUNK DORY'S

A more filling packet of crisps this time, crinkle cut and covered in an incredibly tasty dusting. The buffalo flavour is the one to try. It's the perfect packet for those on the run in need of a snack that will get them over the hump to the next meal.

64 KEOGHS

This family-owned crisp company is located right here in Dublin. Keoghs are extra crispy and come in quite daring flavours like 'Shamrock and Sour Cream' or 'Roast Turkey and Stuffing'. For your sandwich, try the 'Roast beef and Irish stout' flavour. It's excellent, with some bite to it and full of flavour.

65 O'DONNELLS

Proudly gluten-free, these crisps are a hybrid somewhere between a kettle crisp and a Tayto. They come in a number of typical flavours, but the Cheese and Onion and the Hickory Barbeque should be devoured first before anything else. With no artificial ingredients, this is a wonderfully balanced and well-made product.

5 places to find
DELICIOUS
DESSERTS

---

66 **QUEEN OF TARTS**
Cow's Lane, Dame St
Trinity College &
Old City ①
+353 (0)1 633 4681
www.queenoftarts.ie

The chocolate pear and almond tart may be heavy, but it's sensational, as is everything else at this beautifully looking pantry of delights. It's fancier than a lot of other cafes, but the prices are excellent considering the quality.

67 **THE PORT HOUSE IBERICOS**
AT: DUNDRUM TOWN CENTRE
Ballinteer Road
5-6 Pembroke Cottage
South Dublin ⑨
+353 (0)1 216 6133
www.porthouse.ie

There are a lot of delectable tapas to choose from here, and with some nice sangria you can settle comfortably for a long, candle-lit dinner. But at the end of the meal there is only one option: the Ferrero Rocher cheesecake. With its soft cheese, Ferrero Rocher mix and biscuit base, it's everything.

68 **BROTHER HUBBARD**
153 Capel St
O'Connell Street &
the Quays ④
+353 (0)1 441 1112
www.brotherhubbard.ie

All things lovely and crumbly and delicious and crunchy and messy lie within Brother Hubbard. If you have a sweet tooth, don't even try to resist. The brownies are to die for, with flavours like peanut butter and jam or Belgian chocolate... Also try the slices, any of them, all of them. Enjoyment guaranteed.

69 MURPHY'S ICE CREAM

27 Wicklow St
St Stephen's Green &
Grafton St ②
+353 (0)1 86 031 0726
www.murphysicecream.ie

Murphy's have been making their own brand of ice cream for 17 years now in Dingle, Kerry, with a more recent second home in Dublin. There's only two weeks of sunshine in Dublin all year round, but when the sun is finally out, queues are quick to form outside Murphy's. The flavours like Dingle sea salt, Dingle gin, peanut and many more are unbelievable.

70 THE CAKE CAFE

AT: THE DAINTREE BUILDING
Pleasants Place
St Stephen's Green &
Grafton St ②
+353 (0)1 478 9394
www.thecakecafe.ie

This is a great little hidden gem for anyone who loves cakes. From the bulging towers of various chocolate cakes to the more delicate and beautifully crafted fruit cakes: every cake here is a work of edible art. Try the chocolate and Irish stout cake.

70 THE CAKE CAFE

THE BLACK MARKET

105 PLACES
FOR A DRINK

The 5 best
BEER GARDENS

---

71 **THE BARGE**
    42 Charlemont St
    St Stephen's Green &
    Grafton St ②
    +353 (0)1 475 1869
    www.thebarge.ie

Though The Barge has several bars and plenty of disco nights, on a summer's day or night it's the canal right outside the door that brings the big crowds. People are littered everywhere, moving back and forth from the bar, pints in hand. It has an almost music festival buzz.

72 **KIMCHI/HOPHOUSE**
    160 Parnell St
    North Dublin ④
    +353 (0)1 872 8318
    www.hophouse.ie

There's a friendly atmosphere in the Hophouse and the staff are great. The beer garden is a perfect snug little courtyard with about four benches hidden away from the world, everyone huddled together smoking and drinking. The perfect start to the night, and... one of the best Korean restaurants is attached to this bar.

73 PAVILION BAR

Trinity College Green
Trinity College &
Old City ①
+353 (0)1 896 1279
www.ducac.tcdlife.ie/
pavilion

It is a small bar located at one end of a cricket pitch that sells cans/pints mostly to Trinity students but also to tourists and just about everyone when the sun comes out. Depending on the weather, masses of people often spill down the steps and onto and all over the cricket pitch, an oasis of green with a backdrop of Trinity's finest architecture.

74 THE CHURCH

Junction of Mary St
and Jervis St
O'Connell Street &
the Quays ④
+353 (0)1 828 0102
www.thechurch.ie

A converted church that transforms into a club at nighttime. Outside, there is a beer garden that winds around most of the building replete with benches and heaters. The pints are pricy but the food and drinks menu is extensive. There are often barbecues and the beer garden is perfectly located within walking distance of most points of interest.

75 HORSE SHOW HOUSE

34-36 Merrion Road,
Ballsbridge
South Dublin ⑨
+353 (0)1 668 9424
www.horseshowhouse.ie

A classic modern day pub inside, spacious and well lit, with an incredible Aviva stadium lounge and private penthouse area. Outside there is a well kept and wonderfully laid out beer garden with benches for sitting, beer barrels for resting pints, a wood chip floor and garden barbecues if the weather is just right.

The 5 ultimate
SPORTS BARS

---

76 **THE LIVING ROOM**
Cathal Brugha St
O'Connell Street &
the Quays ④
+353 (0)1 872 7169
www.thelivingroom.ie

With a dozen or more screens, pool tables, slot machines, shishas, a pizza shack and a huge beer garden with the biggest screen in the city, this is the mecca when it comes to those important events. Rugby and football world cups draw huge numbers for a lively international crowd.

77 **WOOLSHED BAA & GRILL**
AT: PARNELL CENTRE
Parnell St
North Dublin ④
+353 (0)1 872 4325
www.woolshedbaa.com/
dublin

The Woolshed generally tends to cater for an array of sports: American football, tennis, rugby, football, Irish sports and basketball. With the pitchers of beer and big portions of greasy foods, there is a distinctly American vibe here. Good atmosphere no matter what is being shown.

78 **THE MERCANTILE**
28 Dame St
Trinity College &
Old City ①
+353 (0)1 670 7100
www.mercantile.ie

It's a late night bar. It's a music venue. It's romantic if you make it so and it's rowdy and dark and wonderful to wander around if you like that too. There are a lot of screens and though it tends to fill up quickly on Saturdays, it's always boisterous fun.

79 SINNOTTS BAR

AT: STEPHEN'S GREEN
SHOPPING CENTRE
King St South
St Stephen's Green &
Grafton St ②
+353 (0)1 478 4698
www.sinnotts.ie

As famed for its huge rugby match atmosphere as for its carvery food. Beef, stout and rugby is of course an excellent combination. There's a mix of clientele here – tourists, locals and the sports freaks. Well worth a visit for a good pint and a buzzing atmosphere.

80 THE BACK PAGE

199 Phibsborough Road
North Dublin ④
+353 (0)1 535 5941
www.the-back-page.com

There's the Clubhouse main area for the drinks and *craic* (fun). There's the sports hall for the TV screens and the food. There's the Games Room for ping-pong, board games and video games, and there's the astro green outdoor area with seats and hammocks for enjoying outdoor drinks. It's a brilliant spot.

76 THE LIVING ROOM

5 pubs
OUTSIDE THE CITY CENTRE

81 **JOHNNIE FOX'S PUB**
Glencullen
South Dublin ⑨
+353 (0)1 295 5647
www.jfp.ie

A traditional Irish bar well known for its location: it's the highest pub in Ireland sitting pretty on top of the Dublin mountains. Fox's is almost 220 years old and still provides the welcoming warmth of a turf fire and a fine pint of Guinness. There's live entertainment seven nights a week and a shuttle bus can be arranged through the website.

82 **BOLANDS OF STILLORGAN**
1 The Hill, Stillorgan
South Dublin ⑨
+353 (0)1 210 9760

The interior here is fascinating. It's wall-to-wall with movie memorabilia and every inch of the ceiling is covered with real vinyl LPs – by Elton John, ABBA, The Beatles, you name it. There are plenty of food and drinks options, screens for sports, a pool table upstairs and the Sunday night quiz is just what you need before that Monday morning.

83 THE HOLE IN THE WALL

**Blackhorse Avenue,
Phoenix Park
North Dublin** ⑧
+353 (0)1 838 9491
www.holeinthewall.pub

Located near Phoenix Park, this is a classic Irish pub by all accounts. From the outside it looks like an incredibly long winding building with its white brick and black beams. Inside it's ornate and full of decorations, spacious and yet cosy enough to relax, eat and discover a good wine or a craft beer.

84 JOHN KAVANAGH/ THE GRAVEDIGGERS

**1 Prospect Square,
Botanic Gardens
North Dublin** ⑧
+353 (0)1 830 7978

There's eight generations of the same family behind this pub and it's still going strong since it opened back in 1833.
It's a typical old Irish pub replete with weathered wooden tables, stools, benches and snugs. There's an elegancy in such simplicity that has become synonymous with Irish pubs, and this is one of the finest in the city.

85 THE QUEENS BAR AND STEAK ROOM

**12 Castle St, Dalkey
South Dublin** ⑨
+353 (0)1 285 4569
www.thequeens.ie

Dalkey itself is a sight to see. Established in 1745, The Queens is the drinking and dining epicentre of this picturesque village. Perfect for a sunny day: there's ample dining space out front (it's very popular so book ahead) and a beautiful courtyard to have a drink.

5

CRAFT BEER

pubs

---

86 **P.MAC'S**
30 Stephen St Lower
St Stephen's Green &
Grafton St ②
+353 (0)1 405 3653

P.Mac's is very much a hipster hangout. There is a huge variety of craft beers on offer and the lay-out is quite quirky; miscellaneous furniture, various types of chairs at odds with one another, candlelit ledges and tables. It's dimly, almost romantically lit and is the perfect setting to relax in with friends.

87 **THE PORTERHOUSE CENTRAL**
45-47 Nassau St
Trinity College &
Old City ①
+353 (0)1 677 4180
www.theporterhouse.ie

A very popular spot due in part to its close proximity to Grafton Street and Trinity, but also because it serves up decent food and televises all sports. And if craft beers are what you're here for, there is an extensive menu of almost every conceivable drink including 9% Russian beers, Brain Blasta, Temple Brau and many many more.

88 THE BREW DOCK

**1 Amiens St, Mountjoy
O'Connell Street &
the Quays** ④
+353 (0)1 888 1842
www.galwaybay
brewery.com

One of a long successful chain of Galway microbrewery bars, The Brew Dock has quite a collection to choose from. The Sierra Nevada Hop Hunter is an ale with a good punch and there are a number of outstanding German beers as well as County Armagh's finest MacIvors cider.

89 BEERHOUSE

**84-85 Capel St
North Dublin** ④
+353 (0)1 804 7023
www.beerhouse
dublin.com

Capel Street has a lot to offer these days with brilliant Asian eateries and unique bars. Beerhouse is unmistakable with its arched brickwork outside and its artistic wall art inside. There are 20 beers on tap and a range of Irish and international drinks. There's also lots of cosy sofas, armchairs and a fire. Try a Blue Moon or a Five Lamps, two knockout pints.

90 BLACKBIRD

**82-84 Rathmines
Road Lower
Ranelagh &
Rathmines** ⑦
+353 (0)1 559 1940

All the furniture looks secondhand like you'd find in a Berlin dive bar. And that's a good thing. It's trendy without being overly pretentious and really, it's the best bar going in Rathmines right now. There's plenty of space and many a corner to hide and while away your time. As a side note, try the Galway Hooker on tap: it's wonderful.

5 classic
IRISH PUBS

---

91   **THE BRAZEN HEAD**
20 Bridge St Lower,
Merchants Quay
Trinity College &
Old City ①
+353 (0)1 677 9549
www.brazenhead.com

Dated back to 1198, this is officially Ireland's oldest pub. It's also a particularly attractive pub; from the outside it resembles a small castle or fort with a walkway into a small courtyard with tall stools and bars off to each side. There's a fine pint of Guinness to be had here and some exceptional Irish food. A must-visit.

92   **O'DONOGHUE'S BAR**
15 Suffolk St
St Stephen's Green &
Grafton St ②
+353 (0)1 677 0605
www.odonoghuesbar.ie

A small pub offering brilliant window seats, some fine beers, traditional music and lots of dimly lit corners and tables. It's a perfectly located meeting point within walking distance of all the major shopping areas, ATMs and eateries. And with the Nassau Street bus stops a minute's walk away, it's ideal for that last one for the road.

93 GROGANS

15 William St South
St Stephen's Green &
Grafton St ②
+353 (0)1 677 9320
www.groganspub.ie

Situated right bang in the middle of the creative heart of Dublin, this is the go-to place when the sun comes out on a weekend. The crowds spill out and take over all the available seats and any nearby steps with pints propped up on any ledge or free surface. They also sell fantastic cheese toasties.

94 THE STAG'S HEAD

1 Dame Court
St Stephen's Green &
Grafton St ②
+353 (0)1 679 3687
www.louisfitzgerald.com/
stagshead

The Stag's Head is a real beauty and a fantastically well-preserved Victorian pub. It's all mahogany and granite surfaces, tiled mosaics and soft leather sofa seats. An immensely popular traditional Irish pub, it has won a raft of awards over the years. It's well worth popping by for a pint and investigating all the nooks and crannies.

95 THE LONG HALL

51 Great George's St
South
St Stephen's Green &
Grafton St ②
+353 (0)1 475 1590

From the red brickwork to the beautifully rendered partitions and elaborate wooden panelling, this is another Victorian gem, dating back to 1766. The Long Hall is so named after its long narrow main chamber that opens up into a bigger room at the back. Phil Lynott and Bruce Springsteen, amongst others, were known to enjoy a drink here.

5 bars that
ROCK

---

96 FIBBER MAGEE'S
80-81 Parnel St
North Dublin ④
+353 (0)1 872 2575
www.fibbermagees.ie

A classic rock and metal bar for all ages. The main counter will be lined with the barfly regulars. Beyond which are two pool tables and a small stage where frequently live bands play with ear-piercing ferocity. There is a comfortable sheltered beer garden/smoking area as well.

97 GYPSY ROSE ROCK & BLUES BAR
5 Aston Quay
Temple Bar ③
+353 (0)87 109 4314

If you like hot, sweaty, smelly, hard drinking, hard rocking bars, then this is the one for you. Over its two small floors, there are quieter moments for blues sets but mostly, it's balls-out rock. Expect a very diverse crowd of all shapes and sizes.

98 O'REILLY'S
AT: TARA STREET STATION
2 Poolbeg St
O'Connell Street &
the Quays ④
+353 (0)1 671 6769
www.sublounge.ie

Hidden away down a tiny alley under the Tara Street train station, this medieval looking bar is perfect for a quiet mid-week pint or a rampage come Friday and Saturday nights. Then the cheap drinks and special offers really pull in crowds of all ages and from all walks of life.

99 BRUXELLES

8 Harry St
St Stephen's Green &
Grafton St ②
+353 (0)1 677 5362
www.bruxelles.ie

When you see the Phil Lynott statue, just off Grafton Street, you know you've found Bruxelles. The main bar on the left as you enter offers a typical Irish pub affair but downstairs there are two themed bars. At the end of the stairs, the bar to the right plays mostly indie music and over on the left it's all about hard rock and metal. It's a dark but welcoming place.

100 THE FOGGY DEW

1 Fownes St
Temple Bar ③
+353 (0)1 677 9328
www.thefoggydew.ie

Located at the gateway to Temple Bar at the Central Bank Square, The Foggy Dew has been around since 1901 and has become renowned for its fusion of the modern and the traditional, its friendly atmosphere and its great taste in music. Occasional special live performances on Fridays, and a late night DJ on Saturdays and Sundays are for live music sessions.

99 BRUXELLES

5 pubs we love in
TEMPLE BAR

---

101 GARAGE BAR
10 Essex St East
Temple Bar ③
+353 (0)1 679 6543
www.garagebar.ie

A small but very snazzy bar. It could be just another hipster joint but in the mayhem of the surrounding Temple Bar, it feels like a very genuine oasis of cool. Expect primary colours splashed everywhere and framed album covers on the wall. The prices are just right here and there's a mean cocktail menu.

102 FITZSIMONS
21-22 Wellington Quay
Temple Bar ③
+353 (0)1 677 9315
www.fitzsimonshotel.com

Like most places in Temple Bar, drinking late on a Saturday night isn't cheap here. But Fitzsimons does offer quite a lot: huge screens for sports, several floors that include accommodation, a restaurant, four bars, a nightclub and a roof terrace with a worthy view. Good for larger groups.

103 THE OLD STOREHOUSE
3 Crown Alley
Temple Bar ③
+353 (0)1 607 4003
www.theoldstorehouse.ie

We're into typical Temple Bar tourist territory now. It's big and boisterous with a decent food menu and live music seven nights a week. There's a nice beer garden, lots of little snugs to hide away in and generally there's a good atmosphere here on most weekends.

104 THE SNUG

**15 Stephen St Upper
St Stephen's Green &
Grafton St** ②
+353 (0)1 478 3097

It looks like a giant Doctor Who telephone box shrouded in hanging plants. Even though The Snug is full of knick-knacks to entice the tourists, there is a genuine warmth and cosiness in this dimly lit wood-encased watering hole.

105 HIPPETY'S

**Fownes St Upper
Temple Bar** ③
+353 (0)1 535 7006

Easy to find, Hippety's looks like nothing else in the area. There's a lot of colour outside and the inside is like the Mad Hatter's lair, furnished with an array of bizarre hanging lampshades, dainty tables and chairs and wall art. It's a wine bar, a restaurant and a gallery.

105 HIPPETY'S

The 5 best
PINTS OF GUINNESS
in Dublin

---

106 GUINNESS STOREHOUSE
**St James's Gate
Kilmainham &
Liberties ⑤
+353 (0)1 408 4800
*www.guinness-
storehouse.com***

Unfortunately you can't just walk straight into the Storehouse and start drinking delicious pints of Guinness. It is well worth booking online to avoid the queues and we recommend you take your time and enjoy a full day out here. Alongside the tour and museum there is the Gravity Bar, the Connoisseur Bar, the 1837 Bar & Brasserie and, of course, Arthur's Bar.

107 MULLIGAN'S
**8 Poolberg St
O'Connell Street &
the Quays ④
+353 (0)1 677 5582
*www.mulligans.ie***

Writers Seamus Heaney and James Joyce used to frequent Mulligan's. This classic Dublin pub is so well-known for its Guinness that some have said it's the 'home of the pint'. That's up for debate perhaps. Yet this is a fine establishment to drink a very fine pint indeed.

108 NEARY'S
**1 Chatham St
St Stephen's Green &
Grafton St ②
+353 (0)1 677 8596
*www.nearys.ie***

Neary's has long been associated with the arts due to its close location to the Gaiety Theatre – many famous faces have come through here in the last 130 years. Try and grab the cosy snug through the left-hand door and enjoy a perfect pint of Guinness.

109 **HARTIGAN'S**

100 Leeson St Lower
St Stephen's Green &
Grafton St ②
+353 (0)1 676 2280

There's nothing flash about Hartigan's. There are framed pictures of the good old times and little else in the way of knick-knacks, which is refreshing. It's a plain and simple bar that happens to serve one of the best pints of Guinness in Dublin city.

110 **KEHOE'S**

9 Anne St South
St Stephen's Green &
Grafton St ②
+353 (0)1 677 8312
www.louisfitzgerald.com/
kehoes

Right bang in the heart of Dublin, just off Grafton Street, is this terrific looking and extremely popular pub. Depending on the time of day or night, you may have to stand while drinking, inside or outside, but that's a small sacrifice for the enjoyment of a great pint and the energetic atmosphere.

110 KEHOE'S

5 bars for
TRADITIONAL IRISH MUSIC

---

111 **THE COBBLESTONE**
77 King St North
Smithfield &
Stoneybatter ⑥
+353 (0)1 872 1799
www.cobblestonepub.ie

This fine establishment with the fantastic name calls itself 'a drinking pub with a music problem'. Situated right on Smithfield square, there are a number of places to eat and sleep nearby and for entertainment, well, look no further. There's live music at least three nights a week here.

112 **DEVITTS**
78 Camden St Lower
St Stephen's Green &
Grafton St ②
+353 (0)1 475 3414
www.devittspub.ie

With some of the best local musicians taking part, there are some serious sessions here every Thursday, Friday and Saturday from 9.30 pm. With an array of instruments and guest appearances of locals, the music is always unpredictable and always exciting.

113 **O'DONOGHUE'S PUB**
15 Merrion Row
St Stephen's Green &
Grafton St ②
+353 (0)1 660 7194
www.odonoghues.ie

A range of musicians perform at this legendary spot on Merrion Row, crammed into the bar seven nights a week. Not that long ago, Christy Moore and the Dubliners often played here. If space is a problem, there is a perfect beer garden/ courtyard outside with barrels to prop your drinks on.

114 THE INTERNATIONAL BAR

23 Wicklow St
St Stephen's Green &
Grafton St ②
+353 (0)1 677 9250
www.international-bar.com

The International opened in 1886 and to this day has kept every inch of its ornate Victorian interior intact. Not only is there traditional Irish music but there are jazz nights and comedy club nights, and poetry, spoken word and storytelling on Wednesdays.

115 MCNEILLS PUB

140 Capel St
O'Connell Street &
the Quays ④
+353 (0)1 874 7679

McNeills is a famous traditional Irish music pub with very friendly staff. You never know who's going to turn up and how they will add to the casual sessions that take place every Thursday, Friday and Saturday. A good spot for lunch and a pint or two.

113 O'DONOGHUE'S

5 spots for a
ROMANTIC
drink

116 **ANSEO**
18 Camden St Lower
St Stephen's Green &
Grafton St ②
+353 (0)1 475 1321

Anseo is a small but intimate venue with dimly lit tables in the back, offering romantic couples a chance to have a drink and some private time in a space that also plays great music. If your date stands you up; there is an entire wall of secondhand books you can peruse or purchase.

117 **IDLEWILD BAR**
14 Fade St
St Stephen's Green &
Grafton St ②
+353 (0)1 253 0593
www.idlewilddublin.com

Art Deco meets traditional speakeasy meets tropical cocktail bar; this is Idlewild Bar. Try to get there early and grab the plush green sofas or the small curved corner seats with the individual lamps for added romance. 'Boilermakers' (a shot of whiskey alongside a beer) are a speciality here.

118 **FARRIER & DRAPER**
AT: POWERSCOURT
TOWNHOUSE CENTRE
59 William St South
St Stephen's Green &
Grafton St ②
+353 (0)1 677 1220
www.farrieranddraper.ie

If you want to show off on a date without having to overstretch your budget, Farrier & Draper might just be the perfect place. It's housed in an elegant two-storey Georgian building with multiple rooms, each with their own unique design. There is also a stunning little restaurant attached.

119 THE LIBRARY BAR

AT: THE CENTRAL HOTEL
**1 Exchequer St
St Stephen's Green &
Grafton St ②
+353 (0)1 679 7302
*www.centralhotel
dublin.com***

Take the main entrance at The Central Hotel, head past the reception and then up the stairs to the left, follow it around until you see the sign for the Library Bar. With its large soft leather chairs and charming cases and cabinets of leather-bound books, this is the perfect oasis of quiet to share a drink and watch the city pass below.

120 THE BAR WITH NO NAME

**3 Fade St (underneath the
snail and up the stairs)
St Stephen's Green &
Grafton St ②
+353 (0)87 122 1064
*www.nonamebar
dublin.com***

It has no name but surprise, surprise: 'No Name Bar' (as it is also called) does in fact exist. However, it's not signposted and you might need Google Maps. Once you find it, though, it offers an array of drinks and a wonderful cosy deck to eat/drink out on together.

119 THE LIBRARY BAR

5 tasty
COCKTAIL
joints

---

121 **VINTAGE COCKTAIL CLUB**
15 Crown Alley
Temple Bar ③
+353 (0)1 675 3547
www.vintagecocktail club.com

This very exclusive cocktail bar doesn't look like much from its front door, but that's precisely the point. The hidden world inside offers fine dining, vintage surroundings and candle-lit tables, all very chic and refined. When it comes to Dublin cocktails, this is a secret to know.

122 **37 DAWSON STREET**
37 Dawson St
St Stephen's Green &
Grafton St ②
+353 (0)1 902 2908
www.37dawsonstreet.ie

This is pretty decadent stuff. The place is beautifully designed with incredible art, chandeliers and coloured glass. The cocktails are irresistible of course; the ones infused with chilli and/or egg yolk are a must-try. There's also a respectable food menu and an impressive whiskey bar.

123 **PERUKE & PERIWIG**
31 Dawson St
St Stephen's Green &
Grafton St ②
+353 (0)1 672 7190
www.peruke.ie

Alongside the usual bar drinks and food, Peruke & Periwig is a very highly regarded cocktail joint with an elaborate and inventive menu. Expect classy stuff across two floors, with dapper looking staff and portraitures of all sizes looking down on you. The venue has its very own library bar area as well.

124 THE BLIND PIG

Somewhere Secret, near Grafton St
St Stephen's Green & Grafton St ②
+353 (0)1 565 4700
www.theblindpig.ie

Shhh, this one's a bit of a secret. It's basically an underground cocktail bar reminiscent of the 1920s speakeasies. The catch? It changes location every few months and you must make contact first through e-mail (reservations@theblindpig.ie) and only then will you get directions to find the place. The Blind Pig is the brainchild of award-winning mixologist Paul Lambert.

125 ZOZIMUS

AT: CENTENARY HOUSE
Anne's Lane, Anna St South
St Stephen's Green & Grafton St ②
+353 (0)1 536 9640
www.zozimusbar.ie

The one with the flying umbrellas outside. Wines, cocktails, whiskeys and gins: Zozimus has it all. Some of the cocktails designed in-house though are not to be beaten. Try the Marshmallow Ramos for those with a sweet tooth or the Eucalyptus Flip for something very different.

122 37 DAWSON STREET

125 ZOZIMUS

5

ALTERNATIVE
bars

---

126 THE BERNARD SHAW
11-12 Richmond St South
St Stephen's Green &
Grafton St ②
+353 (0)1 906 0218
www.thebernardshaw.com

It starts with a small door and a small room, a few tables and a bar. Then it continues to a small stairs leading down to the basement opening up onto a dancefloor, bar and DJ booth. Through another door and out into the courtyard you are greeted by with a beer garden, a big blue pizza bus and stunning new food market Eatyard.

127 THE BOWERY
196 Rathmines
Road Lower
Ranelagh &
Rathmines ⑦
+353 (0)85 726 7078
www.thebowery.ie

The Bowery is a bar that looks like a ship. And luckily for all of us who are pirates at heart, there's a substantial rum bar here. Also live music is an integral part of the Bowery experience. A boat, pirates, rum and music... you must admit, it has the makings of a rather unique night. Rock 'n' Rum.

128 MARY'S BAR
8 Wicklow St
St Stephen's Green &
Grafton St ②
+353 (0)1 670 8629
www.marysbar.ie

This bar is also a hardware store with certain non-alcohol-related DIY goods actually on sale. There's a nice little patch to sit in front of the house and at the back there are several basic booths to hide away and drink with friends.

129 THE HACIENDA BAR

15 Little Mary St
O'Connell Street &
the Quays ④
+353 (0)1 873 0535

It's a trendy haunt these days with several celebrity visitors (Hozier being the latest) taking full advantage of the doorbell with very selective access. But if you are let in, you'll find a fairly run-of-the-mill establishment, replete with pool tables and people enjoying the banter with the owner Shay.

130 THE DAWSON LOUNGE

25 Dawson St
St Stephen's Green &
Grafton St ②
+353 (0)1 671 0311

It can't get cosier than this. Dating back to 1850, Dublin's smallest pub has a full seating capacity of 26. Be willing to join in conversation and enjoy the light banter with staff and patrons. It is a unique experience and no visit to Dublin is complete without a pint in here.

126 THE BERNARD SHAW

5 *lively venues for*
CLUBBING

---

131 **YAMAMORI TENGU**
   37 Strand St Great
   O'Connell Street &
   the Quays ④
   +353 (0)1 872 0003
   www.yamamori.ie/
   yamamori-tengu

Top class sushi by day, nightclub by night. There's even a bamboo garden and statuesque buddies and deities watching your every move. But for the greater part, expect banging tracks and merciless flashing lighting. Get there early: it fills up wall-to-wall very quickly.

132 **HANGAR**
   St Andrew's Lane
   St Stephen's Green &
   Grafton St ②
   www.hangardublin.ie

The website is going all Berlin on us proclaiming Hangar feeds off the industrial vibes of what was once a shirt factory. And so be it. Hangar isn't supposed to be fancy. It's all about the lighting and the sounds. Plenty of gigs every week, check the website for details. Book early, because tickets sell out fast and the queues can be lengthy.

133 THE WORKMAN'S CLUB
10 Wellington Quay
Temple Bar ③
+353 (0)1 670 6692
www.theworkmansclub.com

This huge winding multi-room building tends to turn into a sardines-in-a-tin scenario by Saturday night. The music is reliable and there is usually a loud and boisterous atmosphere. There's a huge smoking section/beer garden that offers some welcome relief with slightly fewer people. There are a couple of live gigs here every week too.

134 THE OPIUM ROOMS
26 Wexford St
St Stephen's Green &
Grafton St ②
+353 (0)1 526 7711
www.opiumrooms.ie

Anyone over 35 or on a tight budget might want to leave this one alone. Usually an entrance fee must be paid. But you get six bars over four floors, including a lounge, garden, late bar, restaurant and a main room for showcasing live acts. The Opium Rooms does have a bit of everything.

135 DISTRICT 8
135-138 Francis St
Trinity College &
Old City ①
www.district8dublin.com

This is probably one for a younger crowd: they still have the stamina and bodies capable of dancing in a sweatbox without passing out. It's a top class venue though, that boasts a revolving door of noteworthy DJs and electronic acts. Book ahead.

5 *places to go*
EARLY *in the* MORNING

136 **THE ART OF COFFEE**
AT: IVEAGH COURT
Harcourt Road
St Stephen's Green
& Grafton St ②
+353 (0)1 475 9118
www.theartofcoffee.ie

Monday to Friday the Art of Coffee is open at 7 am for all your tea, coffee, sandwich, porridge and early morning pastry needs. Everything is super fresh and made to order. The coffee is serious stuff and there is such a wide choice that it would be impossible not to find an early morning kick to suit you.

137 **MUNCHIES**
146-A Baggot St Lower
St Stephen's Green
& Grafton St ②
+353 (0)1 661 9168
www.munchies.ie

At 7 am, Monday to Friday, the doors open. There are freshly made buns, breads, pastries, soups, teas and coffees (there's even a take-out flask option for hot drinks that serves up to 10) but most importantly this place is a sandwich-toastie-bagel mecca. So many delicious choices at very good prices! Check their website to find the nearest one to you.

138 SLATTERY'S BAR

129 Capel St
O'Connell Street &
the Quays ④
+353 (0)1 874 6844
www.slatterys.bar

Not always the best or the healthiest choice, but if you're continuing on from the night before or if there's that early morning stag party, Slattery's Early House may be the option for you. Open from 7 am Monday to Saturday, Slattery's has a plethora of traditional Irish food on offer to soak up the pints.

139 THE CHANCERY INN

1 Inns Quay
O'Connell Street &
the Quays ④
+353 (0)1 677 0420

Your typical Irish pub here with a license for that early 7 am start. Some of the early places are quite strict about who they let in at that time of the day, of course, but The Chancery is relatively lenient in this regard. Be warned though; if you were out on a Friday night, you will encounter all kinds of heroes and villains here on a Saturday morning.

140 LOLLY AND COOKS

AT: LIFFEY TRUST CENTRE /
UNIT P
18 Merrion St Upper
St Stephen's Green
& Grafton St ②
+353 (0)1 876 1882
www.lollyandcooks.com

There are five Lolly and Cooks locations but this one opens at 7.30 am Monday to Friday and serves an insanely good take-away breakfast. Bacon and cheddar muffin anyone? Bacon butty? Porridge or breakfast pot? And, of course, there are a lot of coffee and tea options.

5

LITERARY PUBS

---

141 **THE DUKE**
   8-9 Duke St
   St Stephen's Green
   & Grafton St ②
   +353 (0)1 679 9553
   www.thedukedublin.com

Steeped in history, this pub served its first drink way back in 1822. It has long been associated with James Joyce, Patrick Kavanagh and Brendan Behan, but many a pub has a similar claim – these lads got around well enough. These days, it is rather a quiet affair having a pint here.

142 **DAVY BYRNE'S PUB**
   21 Duke St
   St Stephen's Green
   & Grafton St ②
   +353 (0)1 677 5217
   www.davybyrnes.com

The years 1889 to 1914 saw Byrne's become the most celebrated literary pub in Dublin, largely due to the numerous mentions in Joyce's *Ulysses* and *The Dubliners*. Duke Street regulars Behan, Kavanagh and Anthony Cronin, and later Michael Collins and Arthur Griffith all of them drank here at one time or another.

143 **MCDAIDS**
   3 Harry St
   St Stephen's Green
   & Grafton St ②
   +353 (0)1 679 4395

With stained glass and dark wood inside, this is a basic Irish bar. No nonsense, no frills, no extras; you're here to drink in Brendan Behan's and Flann O'Brien's favourite haunt and that's that. Friendly atmosphere and good prices considering its vicinity to Grafton Street.

144 THE BAILEY

1-4 Duke St
St Stephen's Green
& Grafton St ②
+353 (0)1 670 4939
www.baileybarcafe.com

This is the third entry on the same street, with more of the same characters, and we can now add Beckett in here too, and later J.P. Donleavy. It's obvious why all literary tours start and/or end along here. This is also a good spot to celebrate Blooms Day (June 14th) as plenty of Joycean straw hats are handed out then.

145 KENNEDY'S

31-32 Westland Row
Trinity College
& Old City ①
+353 (0)1 679 9077
www.kennedyspub.ie

It's hard to believe Oscar Wilde once stocked the shelves in what used to be a grocer's at this address. It was established as a pub in 1850, and in later years Seamus Heaney loved to drop in for a pint of the black stuff. Architecturally speaking, it's one of the more attractive pubs to drink in, and it's frequented by tourists and students of nearby Trinity College. Good food and proper stout.

5 bars for
WINE & CHEESE

---

146 FALLON & BYRNE
11-17 Exchequer St
St Stephen's Green
& Grafton St ②
+353 (0)1 472 1010
www.fallonandbyrne.com

This place is well known for its beautiful cafe and artisan shopping upstairs, but hidden downstairs is a stunning French brasserie and wine bar. The smell of oak and wines, casks and wisps of faraway cooking immediately hits you as you enter. It's a very classy and comfortable setting with an exceptional wine menu and superb food.

147 LA CAVE
28 Anne St South
St Stephen's Green
& Grafton St ②
+353 (0)1 679 4409
www.lacavewinebar.com

The oldest and one of the best-known French wine bars in Dublin, hidden away from the bustle of the streets. La Cave serves an incredible range of French wines and international favourites plus many lesser-known surprises. The food and the cheese boards are wonderfully French.

148 OLESYA'S
18 Exchequer St
St Stephen's Green
& Grafton St ②
+353 (0)1 672 4087
www.olesyaswinebar.com

It's hard to pass this tantalising spot and not grab one of the tables near the door, or outside, and watch the world pass by. There are 400 wines and a formidable food menu featuring platters of French and Irish cheeses, all sorts of seafood and nibbles, and Siberian ice cream to finish.

149 **ELY WINE BAR**

22 Ely Place
St Stephen's Green
& Grafton St ②
+353 (0)1 676 8986
www.elywinebar.ie

A multiple award winner, Ely Wine Bar has a lot to offer between staff recommendations, wines of the month and a considerable choice of wines by the glass, so you don't have to spend a fortune in such decadent surroundings. Get the Irish and continental cheese board for 2 (9,95 euros) or 4 (19,95 euros).

150 **BAGOTS HUTTON**

6 Ormond Quay Upper
O'Connell Street &
the Quays ④
+353 (0)1 878 8118
www.bagotshutton.com

It's all very hip here. You can tell by the bare brick walls, the art, the colourful seating and the tiny stage for live jazz nights. The food is proper Italian and the pizzas are a firm favourite. We recommend the mountainous meat and cheese board coupled with one of the many wines, champagnes or cocktails on offer.

146 FALLON & BYRNE

5
LGBTQ HOTSPOTS

---

151 **THE HUB**
    23-24 Eustace St
    Temple Bar ③
    +353 (0)1 670 7655

From Thursday to Saturday, The Hub hosts some of Dublin's longest running gay club nights. Expect it to be very crowded and very sweaty. Thursdays are Prhomo (Dublin's gay student night), Fridays are Sweatbox and Saturdays The Hub hosts Mothers. Booking in advance is advised.

152 **THE GEORGE**
    89 Great George's St
    South
    St Stephen's Green
    & Grafton St ②
    +353 (0)1 671 3298
    www.thegeorge.ie

This is usually the first stop for young gay people in Ireland. It is incredibly well known and has a reputation for excellent entertainment seven nights a week. There is a smaller and much quieter section for the older generation, affectionately called 'Jurassic Park'.

153 **STREET 66 DUBLIN**
    33-34 Parliament St
    Temple Bar ③
    +353 (0)1 679 3369
    www.street66.bar

Taking over from renowned gay hangout The Front Lounge comes new venue Street 66 Dublin which draws a very mixed crowd. It serves up some great food and anything that's alcoholic. It's also only a couple of minutes away from Temple Bar.

154 PANTIBAR

7-8 Capel St
O'Connell Street &
the Quays ④
+353 (0)1 874 0710
www.pantibar.com

Home to the one and only Panti Bliss herself, a self-proclaimed 'national fucking treasure'. Keep an eye out for her. This is a very vibrant and flashy bar, full of colourful characters, where kitsch meets modernist cool and everything is lit up in neon red. Great drinks offers and cheaper pints than at most places.

155 SPINSTER

AT: BAD BOBS
35-37 Essex St East
Temple Bar ③
+353 (0)1 677 8860

Another one for the calendar because it doesn't come around very often either. On the third Saturday of every month Bad Bobs hosts a special ladies night roof party to the music of Blondie, the Violent Femmes, Patti Smith, Talking Heads, Cyndi Lauper and so on – the list is endless. Good drinks promos too.

5 fantastic
COFFEE BARS

---

156 **3FE**
32 Grand Canal St Lower
Trinity College &
Old City ①
+353 (0)1 661 9329
www.3fe.com

When someone says 'I want a really good coffee', 3FE is usually the first name that pops up. If you are willing to walk back from the city centre just a little bit, away from the Costas and the Starbucks, 3FE really is worth it. Delicious South American coffees matched with equally delicious donuts.

157 **LEGIT COFFEE CO**
1 Meat Marth, Meath St
Kilmainham &
Liberties ⑤
www.legitcoffeeco.com

Known just as much for its teas and speciality coffees as it is for its brunch and lunch menu. A renovated butcher's, LEGIT looks great too, using a lot of open space and wooden surfaces to establish a comfortable, edgy look all of its own. Try Celbridge's own Baobab coffee and the homemade sausage rolls.

158 LOVE SUPREME COFFEE

57 Manor St
Smithfield &
Stoneybatter ⑥
+353 (0)1 549 6489
www.lovesupreme.ie

This is heaven for any true coffee lover and, typical of Stoneybatter these days, it's also one of the sleekest looking contemporary coffee joints in Dublin. The interior is polished and minimalist with a very clean and clear design. There is a constantly rotating coffee menu every 2-3 months that will focus on a different crop or country each cycle. A second venue has just opened in Portobello.

159 KAPH

31 Drury St
St Stephen's Green &
Grafton St ②
+353 (0)1 613 9030
www.kaph.ie

Similar to Love Supreme is that Kaph is very trendy and hip looking – it also has a very clean minimalist vibe, using only sparse colours. But covering two floors it is certainly the bigger option of the two. Delicious coffee aside, Kaph is also known for its specialty cakes and gluten-free options.

160 IL FORNAIO

15 College Green
Trinity College &
Old City ①
+353 (0)1 671 8960
www.ilfornaiocafe.ie

A beautiful classic-looking Italian eatery and cafe. This is, as they say themselves, 'Italy at your doorstep'. There are meats, oils, pastries and wines, bottles on shelves and in racks, and a sense of community that really creates a warm and friendly atmosphere. Take a seat, relax and drink that very real and very strong Italian coffee.

5 places to enjoy some
PUB GRUB

---

161 **THE BULL & CASTLE BAR**
   5-7 Lord Edward St
   Trinity College &
   Old City ①
   +353 (0)1 475 1122
   www.fxbuckley.ie/
   the-bull-and-castle

You can't go wrong with a good ol' American style bar and restaurant. Bull and Castle's meat is supplied by their own butchers: F.X. Buckley, which is a brand unto itself. They have an excellent reputation for their dedication to their craft and the resulting tenderness and marbling in every slab of beef. There's also a full bar to compliment every dish.

162 **THE OLD SPOT**
   14 Bath Avenue
   South Dublin ⑨
   +353 (0)1 660 5599
   www.theoldspot.ie

Highly recommended in the Michelin 'Eating out in Pubs' Guide of 2016 and 2017, this is so good it feels just like very fine dining... with a bar attached. It's elegant and rustic. It's beers and beef if you like. It's seabass, cheeseboard and cocktails if you like. Either way, this is an exceptional gastropub.

163 THE CHOP HOUSE

2 Shelbourne Road,
Ballsbridge
South Dublin ⑨
+353 (0)1 660 2390
www.thechophouse.ie

The Chop House, another award-winning gastropub, has only one thing on its mind and that's the best possible beef it can source. It is a very relaxed place with soft leather sofas and lots of windows spilling slats of daylight across the wooden floors and bar stools. The menu is exemplary and reads, and tastes, like a Michelin-starred attraction.

164 THE MARKET BAR

14-A Fade St
St Stephen's Green &
Grafton St ②
+353 (0)1 613 9094
www.marketbar.ie

It looks like a giant German beer hall at first glance, but it is in fact a very popular spot for some of the best drinking and tapas in the city, with plenty of gluten-free options. Try the patatas bravas, the enormous portions of nachos, the chicken and chorizo skewers or the calamari, and wash it all down with some delicious cava or sangria.

165 L.MULLIGAN.GROCER

18 Stoneybatter, Arran
Quay
Smithfield &
Stoneybatter ⑥
+353 (0)1 670 9889
www.lmulligangrocer1.
weebly.com

Away from the fancy gastropubs now and back to what resembles your everyday Irish bar. Simply put, at L.Mulligan. Grocer, the basics are just very well executed. It's a homely and comfortable place, there's a huge variety of drinks and the food menu is always evolving. Try the black pudding Scotch egg and the lamb burger if you can. Sensational.

5 bars for
PEOPLE WATCHING

166 TAPHOUSE
60 Ranelagh Road
Ranelagh &
Rathmines ⑦
+353 (0)1 491 3436
www.taphouse.ie

Downstairs is the place to be for a variety of draught and bottled craft beers, alongside all the regular things, in an intimate and friendly setting. Upstairs the balcony has plenty of seats and tables for smoking and drinking, offering the perfect panoptic view to watch all of Ranelagh as it lives and breathes below.

167 CASSIDY'S
27 Westmoreland St
Temple Bar ③
+353 (0)1 670 8604

It's all very Shoreditch here with board games, foosball, graffiti-strewn walls and a selection of quite unique craft beers. But outside, covered by the overhang, is the perfect comfortable spot to sit and watch people passing by on one of the busiest streets in Dublin. Perfect for that creeping eye.

168 THE BANKERS BAR

16 Trinity St
Trinity College &
The Old City ①
+353 (0)1 679 3697
www.thebankersbar.ie

Bankers is a rather elongated bar in the middle of everything at the corner of Trinity street. With Dame Street more or less on one side and Andrew's Lane on the other, come Saturday night, those seats and barrel tables outside are prime positioning for observing the movements of hundreds of people passing by.

169 TRINITY BAR & VENUE

46-49 Dame St
Trinity College &
The Old City ①
+353 (0)1 679 4455
www.trinitybarvenue.ie

This larger than life sports bar is a popular weekend haunt for passing stags and tourists, with live music every night and good reliable food. But outside, sitting with your back to the brick and facing all of Dame Street, is one of the best people watching spots in the city. On a rare sunny day, it's glorious.

170 PYGMALION

AT: POWERSCOURT
TOWNHOUSE CENTRE
59 William St South
St Stephen's Green &
Grafton St ②
+353 (0)1 633 4522
www.pyg.ie

Extremely popular with the college and twenty-something-crowd, Pygmalion serves good cocktails and has an impressive outdoor section taking up most of Coppinger Row. You might have to fight for a seat here but it's not a bad spot to stand and mingle, drink in hand.

5 pubs with
SNUGS

---

171 **TONERS**

139 Baggot St Lower
St Stephen's Green &
Grafton St ②
+353 (0)1 676 3090
www.tonerspub.ie

Toners could quite easily have fit into one of many categories in this book, 'the best pint of Guinness' or 'the best beer garden for instance', but it's the snug here that really makes it. It's the perfect comfortable self-contained wooden stall for a quiet pint or a bit of a rowdy private party.

172 **THE PALACE BAR**

21 Fleet St
Temple Bar ③
+353 (0)1 671 7388
*www.thepalacebar
dublin.com*

A timeless pub and a classic of Victorian architecture, inside and out. Not a lot has changed in its 195-year history. The Palace Bar boasts one of the city's best snugs; pop in the front door and it's on your right at the end of the bar. Even the bar area is divided into sections for a sense of privacy.

173 **WALSH'S**

6-7 Stoneybatter,
Arran Quay
Smithfield &
Stoneybatter ⑥
+353 (0)1 670 8647
www.walshsstoneybatter.ie

This snug feels more plush compared to others. You're treated to shiny lacquered wood and stained glass in a spacious booth. With an outside facing window, the snug is bathed in light in the daytime and as dusk approaches it gets especially cosy.

174 DOHENY & NESBITT

5 Baggot St Lower
St Stephen's Green &
Grafton St ②
+353 (0)1 676 2945
www.dohenyand
nesbitts.ie

It's a beautiful little room with soft leather seats and stools, surrounded on two sides by wooden doors inset with stippled glass. There are no frills here and it can seat scarcely more than six or seven people but when the basics are done well, that's all you need.

175 O'NEILL'S

2 Suffolk St
St Stephen's Green &
Grafton St ②
+353 (0)1 679 3656
www.oneillspub
dublin.com

This is one of the best pubs in the city and much like Toners it could have fitted nicely into any number of other categories (beer garden, craft beers, pub grub) but it has a superb snug if you go through the side door and take an immediate left. Try a pint of Crean's while you're here, a fantastic Irish lager.

175 O'NEILL'S

65 PLACES TO SHOP

5 shops for
BOOK LOVERS

176 CHAPTERS BOOKSTORE
1 Parnell St
North Dublin ④
+353 (0)1 872 3297
www.chapters.ie

Physically speaking, Chapters is Ireland's largest independent bookshop and it can be a bit overwhelming, with its sprawling ground floor selling new books and it's equally sprawling first floor selling second hand books. You'll find books of every variety here and various imprints of the classics at very good prices.

177 THE SECRET BOOK AND RECORD STORE
15-A Wicklow St
St Stephen's Green &
Grafton St ②
+353 (0)1 679 7272

It looks pretty unremarkable from the outside, in fact, it's quite easy to walk past it and not even know it was there. But once you find the doorway and follow the hall, you'll enter into a very cosy and messy book and record shop. If you can sift through the oddities and detritus you might just find some very cheap treasure.

178 DUBRAY BOOKS
36 Grafton St
St Stephen's Green &
Grafton St ②
+353 (0)1 677 5568
www.dubraybooks.ie

This is the Dublin flagship of independent booksellers Dubray Books. There's a lot on offer here and the extremely helpful staff are specialists in their sections and always have plenty of suggestions. After a browse, why not take the stairs up to the brand new cafe and enjoy a coffee.

179 CONNOLLY BOOKS
AT: THE NEW THEATRE
43 Essex St East
Temple Bar ③
+353 (0)1 670 3361
www.thenewtheatre.com

Attached to the New Theatre there is this hip and arty-looking bookshop. Founded in 1932 and named after the republican and socialist leader James Connolly, it sells mostly Marxist material, feminist literature, philosophical and progressive books. A unique bookshop with a great lay-out.

180 THE GUTTER BOOKSHOP
Cow's Lane
Temple Bar ③
+353 (0)1 679 9206
www.gutterbookshop.com

This beautiful bookshop has a little bit of everything on offer. It has a very comfortable welcoming vibe (no stunning bright lights here) and the knowledgeable and friendly staff encourage you to browse as long as you like. The shop is quite open plan with book-lined walls and a number of island displays. They also have a second branch in Dalkey.

179 CONNOLLY BOOKS

5
VINYL
specialists

---

181 INDUB REGGAE STORE

4 Upper Fowens St,
basement
Temple Bar ③
+353 (0)86 076 9495
www.indubreggaestore.ie

InDub Reggae Store is a unique treasure for any reggae fan. It's not the easiest shop to find perhaps, but if you pop through the door that never closes and descend the rickety wooden stairs, beyond the racks of vintage clothes you will come to Ireland's oldest reggae store selling CDs, DVDs and of course vinyl.

182 OLD SCHOOL VINYL RECORD STORE

Swords St
Smithfield &
Stoneybatter ⑥
+353 (0)86 882 4990

The location is a little far from the city centre but if you like electronic music, this is the place for you – the trek might just be worth it. The incredibly informative staff will be happy to do their best to source whatever you need.

183 SPINDIZZY RECORDS

32 Great George's St
South
St Stephen's Green &
Grafton St ②
+353 (0)1 671 1711
www.spindizzyrecords.com

Again, not the biggest store but it does have a fine selection across a multitude of genres – they're best known for their dance section but also have rock from each era, jazz, classical, hip-hop, indie and all that good ol' Irish trad, rock and pop.

184 THE R.A.G.E.

16-B Fade St
St Stephen's Green &
Grafton St ②
+353 (0)1 677 9594
www.therage.ie

Yes, there's vinyl here but there's just so much cool retro computer stuff to geek out over as well (NES, SNES, Sega Megadrive, Game Cubes). As for the vinyl, there's brand new stuff and plenty of reissues ranging from the very commercial to the extremely obscure. It's a great place for a rummage.

185 SOUND CELLAR

47 Nassau St
Trinity College &
Old City ①
+353 (0)1 677 1940

This is a great place to get concert tickets when Ticketmaster has sold out in 2 minutes. It's also a haven for all things rock, serious rock, punk, indie, big hair rock, all things metal, all things loud and gothic and scary and black. It's wall-to-wall music in here and, if you're into that type of music, there's nowhere better.

5 shops for
IRISH SOUVENIRS

---

186 KEVIN & HOWLIN

31 Nassau St
Trinity College &
Old City ①
+353 (0)1 633·4576
www.kevinandhowlin.com

You could head to a Carrolls Irish Gifts and bring home knick-knacks and Leprechaun key rings. Or you could make a little bit of effort and take home some traditional well-made Irish gear. This elegant store has been around for almost 100 years and provides the best in tweed, hats, men's suits and women's jackets.

187 GEORGE'S STREET ARCADE

Great George's St South
St Stephen's Green &
Grafton S ②
+353 (0)1 283 6077
www.georgesstreet
arcade.ie

Less than a 5-minute walk from Grafton Street is this little enclosed Victorian market offering up stalls and independent shops. There's sweets and vinyl and vintage labels, accessories and collectibles, art, flowers and antiques. It's the perfect place for those willing to scrounge for a bargain or haggle for a good deal.

188 HOUSE OF IRELAND

37-38 Nassau St
Trinity College &
Old City ①
+353 (0)1 671 1111
www.houseofireland.com

This is the place to go to for those discerning relatives back at home. Every good Irish brand worth its salt, like Waterford Crystal, John Rocha, Orla Kiely, is represented here, and next to these Irish designers (over 150!) you'll also find some Scottish and English brands.

189 BUTLERS

24 Wicklow St
St Stephen's Green &
Grafton St ②
+353 (0)1 671 0591
www.butlers
chocolates.com

Butlers chocolates are well known for their deep and creamy luxuriousness. The company was established by Marion Butler in the heart of Dublin in 1932. By 1959 the Sorensen family from Cork had bought the business and they have run it to this day. For that perfect gift try any of their boxes or hampers. And for you? Try their sweet thick hot chocolate drink.

190 JAMES FOX CIGAR & WHISKEY STORE

119 Grafton St
St Stephen's Green &
Grafton St ②
+353 (0)1 677 0533
www.jamesfox.ie

The James Fox Store has catered to the lovers of the finer things in life for over 125 years and has acquired quite a name for itself. This is the place to go for Irish and Scottish whiskey and Cuban cigars: there's Oban Distillers Edition whiskey, Teeling's 33-year-old single malt and cigars ranging from Bolivar to Partagas.

5 shops for
VINTAGE SHOPPING

---

191 RHINESTONE JEWELLERS
18 Andrew's St
St Stephen's Green &
Grafton St ②
+353 (0)1 679 0759

Don't expect any rhinestone cowboys but do expect an array of unique vintage rings, necklaces and accessories ranging from simplistic minimalism to sparkling and bejewelled. There's jewellery of all shapes, sizes and prices, both antique and modern, from wedding rings to beautiful gifts for any other occasion.

192 TOLA VINTAGE
10 Fownes St Upper
Temple Bar ③
www.tolavintage.com

This is a very trendy place, full of throwback gear from the recent past, like bomber jackets, Adidas jackets, shirts, dungarees, jumpsuits and lots lots more. The prices are great here and it's a nice friendly spot for a casual dig to see what vintage goodies you can unearth.

193 SIOPAELLA
29 Wicklow St
St Stephen's Green &
Grafton St ②
+353 (0)1 558 1389
www.siopaella.com

Look out for the brick-arched storefront. Siopaella sells second-hand high street goods rather than straightforward vintage pieces, but they have some of those too. It classifies itself as Ireland's largest designer exchange store – a buy-and-sell essentially – with a bit of everything, from Bailey hats to Valentino.

194 THE HARLEQUIN

13 Castle Market
St Stephen's Green &
Grafton St ②
+353 (0)1 671 0202

A small shop with one rack outside and packed to the rafters inside. It's a family-run business with a broad range specialising in clothing from the 1920's to the modern day. There's eveningwear, rock 'n' roll wear, casual outfits and more. Just dive in and see what's there on the day.

195 DUBLIN VINTAGE FACTORY

57 Smithfield Square
Smithfield &
Stoneybatter ⑥
+353 (0)1 872 7144
www.dublinvintage
factory.com

Selling at just 20 euros a kilo, this fantastic looking shop is vintage heaven. Prices are excellent and you'll find a number of big name items here, from Abercrombie and Ralph Lauren shirts to DKNY tops and 80's throwback sweaters.

195 DUBLIN VINTAGE FACTORY

5 great shops for
MEN'S CLOTHES

---

196 THOMAS PINK

29 Dawson St
St Stephen's Green &
Grafton St ②
+353 (0)1 670 3720
www.thomaspink.com

Pink sells accessories, suits, jackets etc, but we're here for their famed shirts, which are immediately eye-catching and very distinct. Prices vary as do the styles – button cuff, double cuff, etc – and the fittings – classic fit, slim fit. If you need a shirt, you need to check out Pink.

197 NOWHERE

65 Aungier St
St Stephen's Green &
Grafton St ②
+353 (0)1 607 8983
www.nowhere.ie

A minimalist-looking store providing only the very best in an exclusive range of men's clothing, footwear and accessories. Expect a newer, bolder type of men's clothing, with edgy alternatives and darker colours, with brands like Nike, Cav Empt and Y-3.

198 INDIGO & CLOTH

9 Essex St East
Temple Bar ③
+353 (0)1 670 6403
www.indigoandcloth.com

Indigo & Cloth is a very cool studio, cafe and store with a very eye-catching front. This boutique has a range of Irish and international brands, designer and high street, and everything else in between – Levi's, Oliver Spencer, Padmore & Barnes, Gitman Vintage, Sandqvist and many more.

199 GENIUS

AT: POWERSCOURT
TOWNHOUSE CENTRE
6-A Clarendon St
St Stephen's Green &
Grafton St ②
+353 (0)1 679 7851
www.genius.ie

For over 25 years now this family-run boutique has existed in Powerscourt Townhouse. Genius is a very cool and slick-looking store with a lot of familiar high-quality brands on sale. The owners visit fashion houses each season to select unique pieces that fit their own aesthetics and please their customers at the same time.

200 TED BAKER

42 Grafton St
St Stephen's Green &
Grafton St ②
+353 (0)1 881 4111
www.tedbaker.com/ie

Ted Baker is a British luxury clothing label with an array of fits for both stylish and casual attire. They also have an entire collection dedicated to very tall men, which is a rarity in Dublin. If you have the cash to spend on something comfortable, perfectly fitted and classic, drop into Ted Baker.

198 INDIGO & CLOTH

5 shops for stunning
WOMEN'S CLOTHES

201 COSTUME

10 Castle Market
St Stephen's Green &
Grafton St ②
+353 (0)1 679 4188
www.costumedublin.ie

Located near Drury Street and the creative centre, this family-run boutique is a clothing landmark for the very fashionable. Prices vary and there is a huge range. Some of the clothes here are simply stunning, by brands like Citrus, Fine, Yves Salomon, Roland Mouret and more.

202 SCOUT

5 Smock Alley Court,
Essex St West
Temple Bar ③
+353 (0)1 677 8846
www.scoutdublin.com

Another of those shops that just look so interesting and beautiful from the outside, you want to have a peek inside. It's a nice roomy store with a lot of colour and warmth. You'll find pieces of knitwear, homewear, footwear and a very carefully curated selection of clothes the owner takes great pride in.

203 TAMP & STITCH

Unit 3 Scarlet Row,
Essex St West
Temple Bar ③
+353 (0)1 515 4705

Tamp is so trendy that it hurts, but the shop looks far too intriguing not to step in and poke around. The jewellery and clothes are carefully chosen to appeal to a certain demographic. If you don't fit this ultra cool demographic, you can still enjoy the wonderful coffee in their boutique cafe.

204 KHAN

15 Rock Hill, Blackrock
South Dublin ⑨
+353 (0)1 278 1646
www.khan.ie

For the discerning shopper with money to burn: we're into big names here. Think Paul Smith, Pierre Balmain, Robert Clergerie and others. Khan has been around since 1994 and they rode out the recession to become a Dublin success story, garnering much acclaim and attention.

205 HAVANA

2 Anglesea House,
Donnybrook Road
South Dublin ⑨
+353 (0)1 260 2707
www.havanaboutique.ie

This very well-known fashion boutique sells one-offs, dresses, skirts, jackets, accessories and more. It offers slightly more unconventional edgy stock than other shops, with designers like Rick Owens, Giorgio Brato, Molly Goddard and Avant Toi. The friendly staff will help you create that perfect casual or formal look.

203 TAMP & STITCH

5 beautiful
INTERIOR DESIGN
shops

---

206 INDUSTRY & CO
41 Drury St
St Stephen's Green &
Grafton St ②
+353 (0)1 613 9111
www.industryandco.com

A beautiful interior design store and cafe all in one, Industry & Co is all about that typical clean minimalist Scandinavian layout. Situated in the middle of Dublin's creative centre, this high-quality and award-winning boutique shop sells a very quirky range of gifts, jewellery, homeware, ceramics and furnishings.

207 STOCK DESIGN
33-34 King St South
St Stephen's Green &
Grafton St ②
+353 (0)1 679 4317

A shop selling many variations of all your everyday items you know you'll need and, to a certain degree, a lot of stuff you didn't know you wanted or needed but you're going to buy now that you've seen it all. Masses of multi-coloured or plain mugs, glasses, vases, utensils, pots and pans.

208 FIND
AT: SAULS COURT / UNIT 1
Cows Lane
Temple Bar ③
+353 (0)1 679 9790
www.findonline.ie

All manner of strange, weird, wonderful and beautiful objects await you in Find. It's a mix of vintage, retro and carefully selected artistic items for your house. It's about the discovery; stumbling upon that unexpected item you can't leave without.

209 ARTICLE
AT: POWERSCOURT
TOWNHOUSE
South William St
St Stephen's Green &
Grafton St ②
+353 (0)1 679 9268
www.articledublin.com

Like Industry & Co above, a lot has been said and written about Article very recently. It's just a very fun shop to walk through with an assortment of knick-knacks, clever gizmos and practical items for the home clearly arranged on the shelves and tables. A great spot for eye-catching contemporary and decorative pieces.

210 MAKERS & BROTHERS
13-15 Saint Clare's
Avenue, Harold's Cross
Ranelagh &
Rathmines ⑦
+353 (0)1 663 8080
www.makersand
brothers.com

With its minimalist one/two-tone objects, smooth edges, straight lines and a practical trendy twist to everyday household goods, Makers & Brothers have a lot of great stuff on offer with a very unique image. There's a lot of emerging talent and small producers on show here.

206 INDUSTRY & CO

209 ARTICLE

The 5 best shops for
IRISH DESIGN

---

211 JAM ART FACTORY

64-65 Patrick Street
Kilmainham &
Liberties ⑤
+353 (0)1 616 5671
www.jamartfactory.com

It looks like a very attractive book or card shop from the outside and there's no actual jam on display but if you want a Ryan Gosling painting – who doesn't? – this is the place to go. The JAF works as an independent art gallery and Irish design shop (showcasing mostly aspiring up and comers with a lot of talent).

212 FOLKSTER

9 Eustace St
Temple Bar ③
+353 (0)1 675 0917
www.folkster.com

There's a lot to explore in Folkster, with new stock coming in all the time. Owned and run by stylists, the place is dripping with ideas and trends making the shop incredibly popular with the rich and fabulous who, like us, want cool unique pieces. The prices vary but most of what's on sale is very reasonably priced.

213 IRISH DESIGN SHOP

41 Drury St
St Stephen's Green &
Grafton St ②
+353 (0)1 679 8871
www.irishdesignshop.com

This shop promised the best of Irish craft and design and for the majority of its nine years in existence, it has fulfilled that promise. Featuring beautifully made homeware, modern and traditional gifts, and prints, the vibe here for useful products rather than knick-knacks.

214 **2ND SPACE**

19 Stephen St Upper
St Stephen's Green &
Grafton St ②
+353 (0)1 679 1211

A partner in crime to the original flagship Om Diva, 2nd SPACE is relatively new and generating a bit of buzz at the moment. It's all very tasteful, colourful, affordable vintage clothing with the aim of promoting emerging Irish designers while at the same time injecting fun and experimentation back into clothes away from familiar prints and motifs.

215 **DESIGNIST**

68 Great George's St
South
St Stephen's Green &
Grafton St ②
+353 (0)1 475 8534
www.shop.designist.ie

The best of Irish design, in the form of household products and all sorts of gifts, like soaps and gadgets, mugs and humourous books or backpacks, and also beautiful stationery like greeting cards, great little notebooks and folding rulers. Absolutely worth a visit for that perfectly suited quirky yet useful gift.

215 DESIGNIST

5 shops you shouldn't miss on
GRAFTON STREET

---

216 THE DECENT CIGAR EMPORIUM

46 Grafton St
St Stephen's Green &
Grafton St ②
+353 (0)1 671 6451
www.decent-cigar.com

It's not an easy shop to find at first, so look up and look out for the signpost. The cigars here come from all over the world (Honduras, Jamaica, Cuba, the Dominican Republic, …) and the guys selling them really know their stuff. There's also the Havana Cafe to enjoy real Cuban coffee and cigars in a very relaxed atmosphere.

217 GINO'S GELATO

34-B Grafton St
St Stephen's Green &
Grafton St ②
+353 (0)1 633 6848
www.ginosgelato.com

Why wait until the Summer? Gino's rich and creamy ice cream is good enough to eat any day of the year. Gino's has several locations in the city centre and the gelato is genuinely exceptional (and made by trained hands early every single morning). There's also coffee, crepes and waffles.

218 CAMERA CENTRE DUBLIN

56 Grafton St
St Stephen's Green &
Grafton St ②
+353 (0)1 677 5594
www.camera.ie

Founded in 1971, this family-run business has become the mecca of all things camera related. You name it, they've got it; printers and drones, optics, lenses, bags and tripods. They do repairs and they give great advice: these are people who really know their products.

219 **SPACE NK**

82 Grafton St
St Stephen's Green &
Grafton St ②
+353 (0)1 677 8616
www.spacenk.com

It's good to see something a little different on Grafton Street that provides more than just clothes. Space.NK.apothecary is a beauty shop tailored to both men and women with an extensive range of products to suit every wallet. The selection here also includes wellness and sun and travel products.

220 **WEIR & SONS**

96-99 Grafton St
St Stephen's Green &
Grafton St ②
+353 (0)1 677 9678
www.weirandsons.ie

Established in 1869, Weir & Sons has become well recognised as one of the best places to go for engagement rings, watches, repairs or for that elegant present. This is a dedicated family-run business that operates with impeccable customer service and a thorough knowledge of their products.

5 tempting
SWEET SHOPS

---

221 CANDY LAB
Cope St, junction of
Fownes St Upper
Temple Bar ③
+353 (0)1 559 7431
www.candylab.ie

This small but impressive shop features just about every ultra sugary item you've ever heard of. From Pop Tarts to Gobstoppers to Kool-Aid and Hershey's, or retro candies of years gone by, it's all there. For the perfect cinema munch, try the salty and sweet M&M's Snack Mix bags. A revelation.

222 SWEET MOMENTS
AT: DUN LAOGHAIRE
SHOPPING CENTRE
Marine Road
South Dublin ⑨
+353 (0)89 959 9549
www.sweetmoments.ie

Tucked away on the ground floor of Dun Laoghaire shopping centre lies this sugary beast just waiting to gobble your money. Similar to some of the other shops listed, Sweet Moments is a mix of old and new, sweet and sour, sugar and salt, but they also specialise in rare and unusual Irish treats.

223 MR TREATS SWEETS
2 Crown Alley
Temple Bar ③
+353 (0)85 765 9406
www.mrtreatssweets.
wix.com

Mr Treats Sweets has only been around since 2010 but it has caught up with all the competition by providing a time warp back to the age of sweets in jars, sticky fingers and brown paper bags. Open seven days a week. Just follow the sign and the stairs on Crown Alley.

224 MR SIMMS OLDE SWEET SHOPPE

59 Dame St
Trinity College &
Old City ①
+353 (0)1 677 4667

A serious throw-back to the sweet shops of our youth, with over 6000 classic products. The shop is literally wall-to-wall with bottles and jars of all the old favourites like sherbet dips, popping candy, jellies, blackjacks, rhubarb and custard or lemon bonbons, and there's also an assortment of modern goodies.

225 AUNTIE NELLIE'S

17-A, Temple Bar
Temple Bar ③
+353 (0)87 345 2665
www.auntynellies.ie

As if Temple Bar needed more temptation, then along comes this rather fetching looking shop. Inside you're surrounded wall-to-wall by a mix of all those Irish/English greats as well as those American favourites (they have Twinkies, Reese's, Red Vines). Try the chocolate frogs and the butter fudge.

5
ALTERNATIVE *shops* TO EXPLORE

226 TEA GARDEN

7 Ormond Quay Lower
O'Connell Street &
the Quays ④
+353 (0)86 219 1010
www.tea-garden.eu

Swap your cafes and pubs for something
a little different and enjoy tea by the cup
or by the pot, be it black, white, green
or oolong, in a laid-back atmosphere.
Most of the rooms are filled with soft
colours, a scattering of cushions for your
arrangement on the floor and a candle-
lit table or two, or if you prefer; there
is a menu of teas and teapots for sale to
takeaway with you.

227 PARJUMARIJA
AT: THE WESTBURY MALL

25 Clarendon St
St Stephen's Green &
Grafton St ②
+353 (0)1 671 0255
www.parfumarija.com

This fascinating and very chic looking
specialist shop is an awakening of the
senses and home to a range of rare
fragrances. Away from the world of
commercial mass produced products,
owner Marija Aslimoska has selected very
specific perfumes that contain some of the
rarest and most unique ingredients.

228 ULYSSES RARE BOOKS

10 Duke St
St Stephen's Green &
Grafton St ②
+353 (0)1 671 8676
www.rarebooks.ie

If you're a book lover or even a passer-by intrigued by the window display, this is a wondrous shop to spend time in. There are all sorts of rarities and oddities across a huge range of prices. There are first/early editions and signed copies of a number of beloved books by authors as diverse as James Joyce, Jules Verne, Lewis Carroll, Haruki Murakami, Philip K. Dick and more.

229 PICADO MEXICAN PANTRY

44-A Richmond St
South
Ranelagh &
Rathmines ⑦
+353 (0)1 479 2004
www.picadomexican.com

There are a number of food items on sale in Picado that are impossible to find anywhere else, like horchata, proper salsa verde, fragrant dried chillies, and other things that you didn't think you needed but you absolutely do. Try the incredible Ibarra Drinking Chocolate. Cooking classes and workshops are available but book fast, they are in very high demand.

230 APASSIONATA FLOWERS

29 Drury St
St Stephen's Green &
Grafton St ②
+353 (0)1 672 9425
www.appassionata.ie

You don't have to be a plant or flower person to appreciate the elegance of Apassionata Flowers. This dainty little store has a fine selection of extraordinary terrariums, orchids, cacti, venus flytraps, blooms and bouquets. Their service is first rate and the staff are more than happy to answer any of your questions.

The 5 most special shops in the
POWERSCOURT
TOWNHOUSE CENTRE

59 William St South
St Stephen's Green & Grafton St ②
+353 (0)1 679 4144

231 THE BONSAI SHOP
+353 (0)1 679 3456
www.bonsaishop.ie

This is the only shop that deals exclusively with all things bonsai. Maureen Massey has run this shop for over 30 years and caters to all bonsai needs – styling, pruning, wiring, repotting – with extensive knowledge and experience. There are workshops in spring and autumn.

232 BARK & BERRY
+353 (0)1 679 8269
www.barkandberry.ie

Bark & Berry is first and foremost a home fragrances shop selling a wide range of luxury brand Dr. Vranjes sprays, wicks, candles and decanters. But this elegant home away from home also sells a small but exquisite selection of household goods and furnishings.

233 JEAN CRONIN VINTAGE & CONTEMPORARY

+353 (0)86 824 6867
www.jeancronin.com

The name says it all; Jean Cronin is a mix of old and new and everything in between. Pick an era or two and mix and match. Cluster those 1950's earrings to that 1970's sequin dress and take along the beaded bag from the 1920's.

234 KID

+353 (0)1 535 1876
www.kidstoredublin.com

KID is definitely a cool kids store, with its minimalist white-washed, almost factory-like, vibe. Located on the top floor of Powerscourt, KID houses collections of very contemporary, very well-made children's clothing and accessories. Super trendy with plenty of fabulous prints and designs.

235 MADE

+353 (0)1 555 4644
www.madedublin.com

Powerscourt Townhouse is home to a number of *über* trendy spots and concept store Made is one such place. Its use of space and white surfaces showcasing the clothes, jewellery, bags etcetera, all displayed rather starkly, makes for a very striking look. Everything here has been selected with great care from a number of Irish and European designers.

5

MARKETS

where you'll want to spend hours

236 **BLACKROCK MARKET**

19-A Main St, Blackrock
South Dublin ⑨
+353 (0)1 283 3522
www.blackrock
market.com

Situated down a narrow little lane that opens out into a maze of little courtyards and stalls, Blackrock Market is clobbered together by a number of sellers peddling second-hand books, artwork, fantastic food, coins, fortune telling, furnishings and all manner of knick-knacks. Open to all, on Saturdays, Sundays and Bank Holiday Mondays.

237 **LIBERTY MARKET**

71 Meath St,
Merchants Quay
Kilmainham &
Liberties ⑤
+353 (0)1 280 8683
www.libertymarket.ie

A famous market and one of Dublin's longest running, the Liberty Market sells just about everything, from engravings to gardening tools to books and toys. There are superb bargains to be found here and there's a very friendly international feel thanks to its city centre location. The website also allows you to shop online.

238 PEOPLE'S PARK FARMERS MARKET

Park Road,
Dún Laoghaire
South Dublin ⑨
www.dunlaoire.com/
sundaymarket.html

Every Sunday without fail this Park Market draws the crowds. A lot of that has to do with its close proximity to the sea, the pier/dog walkers and the famous Teddy's Ice Cream shop, but of course the stalls here are another huge reason. They cover everything from your typical BBQ fare to Asian foods, sauces, cheeses and baked goods, sweets and cakes (the most popular stand of the lot always seems to be the falafels) to second-hand books, plants, landscape photography and crafts.

239 HOWTH FARMERS MARKET

3 Harbour Road, Howth
North Dublin ⑧
+353 (0)1 839 4141
www.howthmarket.ie

Located out in the beautiful coastal town of Howth, Howth Market is on every weekend, showcasing local foods and design, with artisanal goods from near and far. There are five permanent shops and then a revolving series of stalls serving hot gourmet lunches, sandwiches and cakes and treats.

240 HA'PENNY FLEA MARKET
AT: THE GRAND SOCIAL

35 Liffey St Lower
O'Connell Street &
the Quays ④
+353 (0)1 873 4332
www.thegrandsocial.ie/
market

The Grand Social is a great venue for drinks and music in its own right, but every Saturday from noon until 6 pm, it hosts an indoor market on its ground floor. Local craftspeople and designers of all kinds are welcomed alongside a number of representatives from some of the city's shops. A good spot to find interesting vinyls and antiques.

THE THIN BUILDING

30 BUILDINGS TO ADMIRE

---

5 lasting examples of
GEORGIAN
ARCHITECTURE

---

241 THE DOORS OF DUBLIN

Merrion Sq/Fitzwilliam
Sq/Baggot St
St Stephen's Green &
Grafton St ②

Wondering why there are so many brightly coloured Georgian doors in Dublin's city centre? The truth is quite boring so we'll stick to the myth here about writer George Moore and his friend and neighbour Oliver St. John Gogarty. On his drunken ramblings, Gogarty could never find his own door and always knocked on Moore's. So Moore decided to paint his green to avoid confusion and in return Gogarty painted his red. And from there it continued.

242 NUMBER TWENTY NINE

29 Fitzwilliam St Lower
St Stephen's Green &
Grafton St ②
+353 (0)1 702 6163
www.number
twentynine.ie

This Georgian House Museum is perfectly preserved and immaculately furnished to look exactly as it would have between the years 1790-1820. It's a perfect attraction for a rainy day: get inside, feel the history and allow yourself to be taken back to life in an elegant townhouse.

243 HENRIETTA STREET

North Dublin ④

This is supposedly the first Georgian street built in Dublin city centre. From its example, many other buildings and streets followed suit in much the same style and layout. It was an extremely sought after address in the 18th century. Number 14 will be opening as a Tenement Museum later in 2017.

244 THE 5 GEORGIAN SQUARES

St Stephen's Green & Grafton St ②

North Dublin ④

Mountjoy and Parnell on the northside, Merrion, Fitzwilliam and St. Stephen's Green on the southside are the five Georgian squares that together comprise a considerable chunk of Dublin architectural history. The buildings and the small parks they encompass are of huge historical significance and an attraction to tourists and nationals alike.

245 O'CONNELL STREET

O'Connell Street & the Quays ④

Initially this was a street like any other but in the 18th century it was rebuilt and vastly improved. The roads and the paths were expanded and one of Dublin's greatest landmarks, the General Post Office, opened here in 1818. Subsequently, before it became a mecca for shopping, eating and drinking, it was the epicentre of the 1916 Easter Rising.

5 *memorable*
BRIDGES
to cross

---

246 HA'PENNY BRIDGE

Linking Bachelors Walk (North) to Merchant's Arch (South)
O'Connell Street & the Quays ④

This cast iron pedestrian bridge was built in 1816 traversing the River Liffey. The bridge replaced the ferries used to bring people from the south side to the north side of the river and back again. Originally there was a toll (of a ha-penny) to use the bridge but it's long gone now.

247 EAST-LINK TOLL BRIDGE
AKA THOMAS CLARKE BRIDGE

East-Link Toll Plaza, York Road
Linking North Wall to Ringsend
South Dublin ⑨

This bridge has been in operation since 1984 and, just like the Ha-penny Bridge, it replaced the need for cross-river ferries. It's a bascule-type lifting bridge that separates in the middle and parts upwards halting traffic and allowing boats to pass through. Nowadays, heading north or south via this bridge, all vehicles must pay a toll.

248 SEÁN O'CASEY BRIDGE

Linking City Quay (South) to North Wall Quay
South Dublin ⑨

This relatively modern swing bridge opened in 2005 for pedestrians and cyclists. It looks fantastic lit up at night with its rows of floor lights. It's fascinating watching the swing movement in operation, which only happens for large ships to pass or for maintenance; the two legs swivel and pull the bridge apart, each half lining up parallel to the quays.

249 ANNA LIVIA BRIDGE
Linking Lucan Road to
Chapelizod Road
North Dublin ⑧

Here's a good old-fashioned, three-arched, four-legged stone bridge that has spanned the River Liffey since 1753. It was named after the character Anna Livia Plurabelle from James Joyce's baffling novel *Finnegan's Wake*. In the book she is described as the river woman and hence she's the personification of the river itself.

250 SYNOD HALL BRIDGE
Over Winetavern St
Trinity College &
Old City ①

Linking Christ Church to Dublinia over the traffic of Winetavern Street this bridge is unlike the others in this list as it's an enclosed bridge. It's short but it's a really beautiful and unique piece of work. On each side there are circular and angular stained glass windows and there's a vaulted roof with arching high beams.

250 SYNOD HALL BRIDGE

5

CHURCHES

to investigate

---

251 ST MICHAN'S CHURCH
Church St, Arran Quay
O'Connell Street &
the Quays ④
+353 (0)1 872 4154

Founded in 1095 by the Danes, this church has a very interesting crypt, with coffins scattered everywhere. The four central mummies, estimated to be between 400 to 800 years old, are known as The Unknown, The Thief, The Nun and The Crusader. Guided tours are available.

252 ST ANN'S CHURCH
Dawson St
St Stephen's Green &
Grafton St ②
+353 (0)1 676 7727
www.stann.dublin.
anglican.org

It may be easy to miss this Protestant church on such a busy and central street like Dawson Street. But inside it's quite beautiful. Bram Stoker (author of *Dracula*) and Theobald Wolfe Tone (founding father of the Republican movement in Ireland) were both married here (not to each other).

**253 CHURCH OF
ST NICHOLAS OF MYRA**
Francis St
Kilmainham &
Liberties ⑤
+353 (0)1 453 0387
www.francisstreetparish.ie

From the outside it looks like a huge tomb or shrine, but inside it's a deceptively large church where mass is held seven days a week. There's a beautifully ornate altar and nave. The ceiling features the Manx emblem of the Isle of Man, as a reminder that the Isle was once part of the parish of Francis Street.

254 ST AUDOEN'S CHURCH

High St, Merchants
Quay
Trinity College &
Old City ①
+353 (0)87 239 3235
www.heritageireland.ie/
en/dublin/staudoenschurch

No doubt one of the most overlooked attractions in Dublin. This stunning stone fortification looks more like a castle than any church, replete with towers and a bell dating back to Norman times. A low archway leads through Dublin's original city walls and up the forty steps to the gate. Rumours have it that St. Audoen's is haunted by the mysterious Green Lady ghost.

255 CHRIST CHURCH CATHEDRAL

Christchurch Place,
Wood Quay
Trinity College &
Old City ①
+353 (0)1 677 8099
www.christchurch
cathedral.ie

Founded in the 11th century by a Norse king, Christ Church was at first a Viking church then an Irish church. There are daily services but also a number of events each month. Beneath it lies Ireland's biggest medieval crypt with a number of relics, a piece of Jesus' crib and the mummified remains of a cat and a rat.

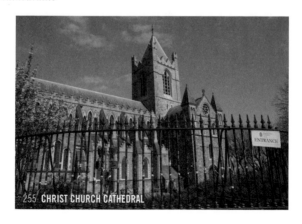

255 CHRIST CHURCH CATHEDRAL

5
UNUSUAL BUILDINGS
to look out for

—————

256 **THE THIN BUILDING**
9 College Green, Dame St
Trinity College &
Old City ①

This mysterious brown brick building on Dame Street a couple of doors up from the Central Bank is almost as tall as the buildings on either side of it, but only wide enough to allow a front door and a plaque with a ship motive over the doorframe. Made of nothing but pure brick all the way to the roof, it is entirely windowless.

257 **CASINO AT MARINO**
Cherrymount Crescent,
off the Malahide Road,
Marino
North Dublin ⑧
+353 (0)1 833 1618
www.casinomarino.ie

Here's a classic example of neoclassical architecture in Ireland. It was designed as a pleasure house by the widely celebrated Scottish architect Sir William Chambers for James Caulfeild, the first Earl of Charlemont. Inside is not at all what one would expect. Across three floors there are sixteen ornate rooms including a vestibule and a state bedroom (with pillars).

258 KIOSK

56 Adelaide Road
St Stephen's Green &
Grafton St ②

This is the tiny little brick landmark with the red and white awning and hanging baskets you might drive by on your way in and out of the city centre, as it's situated at the intersection of a number of roads. At first it was a water pressure station, then a public toilets and now it is a cafe.

259 FREEMASONS' HALL OF DUBLIN

17-19 Molesworth St
St. Stephen's Green &
Grafton Street ②
+353 (0)1 676 1337
www.freemason.ie

This Dublin Hall is the governing body of all the Freemasons lodges across Ireland. Pictures of the interior are, to say the least, astonishing, with immaculate chambers and black and white tiled floors or royal red carpets, walls festooned with emblems, artefacts and relics of all kinds. Email for more information.

260 HELL FIRE CLUB

Montpelier Hill
South Dublin ⑨

This was once a hunting lodge, home to the Hell Fire Club society. Built on an ancient burial site, it was cursed from the outset and all kinds of horrific tales about it have been told. It became a hangout for various societies, drinkers and gamblers with the devil himself even appearing at one infamous card game.

5 buildings that show the city's
MODERN SIDE

261 **BORD GÁIS ENERGY THEATRE**

Grand Canal Square, Docklands
O'Connell Street & the Quays ④
+353 (0)1 677 7999
www.bordgaisenergytheatre.ie

Designed by Daniel Libeskind and opened in 2010, this theatre holds just over 2000 people and hosts some of the biggest shows touring the world. Situated in the Grand Canal Dock with its slanted roof and angular glass construct it looks extraordinary, particularly at night when the theatre and its surroundings are lit up by a series of multicoloured lights.

262 **SAMUEL BECKETT BRIDGE**

Linking Sir John Rogerson's Quay (South) to the Docklands (North)
O'Connell Street & the Quays ④
www.bridgesofdublin.ie/ bridges/samuel-beckett-bridge

Designed in the shape of a harp and dedicated to the Nobel Prize winning playwright Samuel Beckett, this bridge was built in 2009 and fitted in perfectly with the modernisation of the Docklands area. The bridge says as much about the area as it does about the man who inspired it: Beckett challenged and reworked the written word into new forms, just like this bridge challenges our ideas of what a bridge could and should look like.

263 **LIGHT HOUSE CINEMA**
Market Square,
Smithfield
Smithfield &
Stoneybatter ⑥
+353 (0)1 872 8006
www.lighthousecinema.ie

This newest and boldest arthouse cinema in Ireland finally opened its doors in 2012 in the vibrant Smithfield area of Dublin. In a spacious and brightly coloured interior you can watch a mix of commercial and exclusive international films. Many of the Dublin Film Festival screenings are also played here.

264 **TRINITY LONG ROOM HUB**
Trinity College grounds,
Fellows' Square
Trinity College &
Old City ①
+353 (0)1 896 3174
*www.tcd.ie/trinity
longroomhub*

The building of the Arts and Humanities at Trinity looks like a series of panels that may once have formed a solid block but somehow have now shifted out of place, leaving frameless glazed ice blue windows in various spots. Surrounded by more classical structures, it's meant to remind us of the past as well as the future.

265 **CONVENTION CENTRE DUBLIN**
Spencer Dock,
North Wall Quay
O'Connell Street &
the Quays ④
+353 (0)1 856 0000
www.theccd.ie

Since its opening in 2010 the CCD has hosted over 14.000 events, and it has won a number of awards along the way. There's certainly no way to miss this building along the quays, with its cylindrical shape and immense size (basically it looks like the leaning coke can of Dublin). At night-time it's lit up with bands of bright neon colours.

The 5 most
IMPORTANT BUILDINGS

266 GPO (GENERAL POST OFFICE)
O'Connell St Lower
O'Connell Street &
the Quays ④
+353 (0)1 872 1916
www.gpowitnesshistory.ie

The General Post Office has been the headquarters of the Irish Post Office since it opened in 1818, but it's most famous for serving as the headquarters for the leaders of the 1916 Easter Rising. Destroyed by fire and rebuilt, very little of the original building still remains. There is a GPO Witness History tour can be booked online.

267 LEINSTER HOUSE
Kildare St
St Stephen's Green &
Grafton St ②
+353 (0)1 618 3271
www.oireachtas.ie/par-liament

Leinster House has been the seat of the Oireachtas (the Houses of Parliament) since 1922. It consists of Dáil Éireann (the Lower House) and Seanad Éireann (the Upper House). You can book a walk-up guided tour throughout the year on Mondays and Fridays at 10.30 am and 2.30 pm if the House is not sitting.

268 THE FOUR COURTS
Inns Quay
O'Connell Street &
the Quays ④
+353 (0)1 888 6000
www.courts.ie

The Supreme Court, the High Court and the Dublin Circuit Court are all housed in this building (The fourth court is the Central Criminal Court but it no longer exists there). The Four Courts was central to the 1916 Easter Rising and was almost completely destroyed in the 1922 Civil War.

269 THE CUSTOM HOUSE

North Dock
O'Connell Street &
the Quays ④
+353 (0)1 888 2000
www.housing.gov.ie

A masterpiece of 18th-century neoclassical architecture, the Custom House is home to the Department of Housing, Planning and Local Government. It's one of the most impressive buildings in Dublin so you may just want to stand outside and take pictures, but there is a visitor centre and a free historical exhibition inside as well.

270 DUBLIN CASTLE

Dame St
Trinity College &
Old City ①
+353 (0)1 645 8813
www.dublincastle.ie

This is a must-see if you come to Dublin. Make time for it, because there is a lot to appreciate here. The castle hosts a number of events around the year including temporary exhibitions but it also has its own permanent tour, open daily, that includes a throne room, a number of state apartments and a collection of decorative art and priceless artefacts.

269 THE CUSTOM HOUSE

THE GARDEN OF REMEMBRANCE

95 PLACES TO DISCOVER DUBLIN

5 famous
SEATS

271 THE HUNGRY TREE

The King's Inns,
Constitution Hill,
Inns Quay
North Dublin ④

Yes, of course trees need food too, but it's just unusual one would choose to devour a bench. Over many many years this large and Heritage protected London Plane tree has grown in and around the bench literally consuming it and creating a fantastic photo opportunity.

272 WITTGENSTEIN'S STEPS

The Great Palm House
at the National
Botanical Gardens
North Dublin ⑧
+353 (0)1 804 0300
www.botanicgardens.ie

The Botanical Gardens are a stunning place to wander around, weather permitting, but for those looking for some celebrity value to their trip: the famous philosopher Ludwig Wittgenstein lived and worked in Dublin for two years in the 1940s. He could often be found sitting and writing on the front steps at the Palm House.

273 SAMUEL BECKETT'S BENCH

Foxrock Village
South Dublin ⑨

It's only fair that the genius behind *Waiting for Godot*, *Endgame*, *Come and Go*, and *Krapp's Last Tape* should have a permanent commemorative piece in his name in Foxrock. After all, he was born here in 1906. In memory there is a plaque and two inscribed seats.

274 PATRICK KAVANAGH

Wilton Terrace
Grand Canal Dock
South Dublin ⑨

Besides this bronze bench of man and seat fused together, there is also a simple Kavanagh seat on the south bank at the Lock Gates of the Baggot Street Bridge. And then there's the third seat, another fused man and seat memorial, outside the Raglan Road pub in Disneyland, Orlando Florida.

275 HASLAM MEMORIAL SEAT

St Stephen's Green
St Stephen's Green &
Grafton St ②

Anna and Thomas Haslam were the founding members of the Dublin Women's Suffrage Association in 1876. Anna was a hugely popular feminist rights campaigner and was pivotal in achieving the right to vote for women. Thomas wrote and published *The Woman's Advocate* in 1874. The inscription on the seat is dedicated to their many years of devotion to a worthy cause.

271 THE HUNGRY TREE

5

PEACEFUL
places to **RELAX**

---

276 **ROSE GARDEN**

Trinity College,
College Green
Trinity College &
Old City ①

The rose garden might be small but it's beautifully kept. There is a meditative quality to the simplicity of rough wooden benches, each etched with a dedication to someone, shrouded by fragile plants and creeping greenery and dotted rose bushes.

277 **HODGES FIGGIS**

56-58 Dawson St
St Stephen's Green &
Grafton St ②
+353 (0)1 677 4754
www.waterstones.com/
bookshops/hodges-figgis

Owned by Waterstones, Hodges Figgis is a titan when it comes to bookshops. There are a lot of floors here with a lot to choose from. The comfy armchairs on the second floor in the history and ancient classics section are an added bonus for anyone who wants to relax and pick over a few selections, dream a little about where to go to next or maybe just get out of the rain.

278 **ST KEVINS PARK**

8 Camden Row
St Stephen's Green &
Grafton St ②

The 13th-century St Kevins Park is located off Wexford Street, bordered by high walls and accessible through a small gate. It's the perfect place for a quiet sit down amidst the abundance of greenery, or for a leisurely walk in and around the historical church and graveyard.

279 **THE CLOCKWORK DOOR**

51 Wellington Quay
(first floor)
Temple Bar ③
+353 (0)1 538 0998
www.clockworkdoor.ie

A home away from home, The Clockwork Door has only existed for a few months but it's quite an incredible project. Also known as Dublin's first 'Time House', it is a multi-room venue where you can pay to enjoy the space and Wi-Fi with unlimited tea, coffee and biscuits, meet people, hang out and play games or use the study room. Keep an eye out for regular events.

280 **THE DOG HOUSE BLUES TEAROOM**

Howth DART Station,
Howth Road
North Dublin ⑧
+353 (0)1 839 5188
www.thedoghouse
howth.com

Once you step out of Howth DART Station, take a sharp turn right and you'll come upon a ramshackle gathering of assorted tables and chairs in a very comfortable outdoor setting. You can lounge outside at one of the large mahogany dining room tables over a pot of tea, or you can pop indoors for some excellent pizza

Dublin's 5
ISLANDS

---

281 DALKEY ISLAND
Dalkey
South East Dublin
www.dalkeycastle.com/
news-events/ferry-trips-
dalkey-island

Tiny Dalkey Island is a mere 9 hectares and can be reached by boat if you book ahead. It's rather flat and beside a Martello Tower, there's not a lot here to explore but on a sunny day it is an incredible spot to picnic and have a drink. It's only a 5-minute journey from Coliemore Harbour.

282 SKERRIES ISLANDS
Skerries
North East Dublin
www.skerriesseatours.ie/
trips.html

Further north from Lambay Island and about 1,5 kilometre east of Skerries lie the three Skerries Islands: Shenick's, St Patrick's and Colt. The latter two can only be reached by boat, but Shenick's is easy to access via the sand flats at low tide. All three are home to many species of birds.

283 BULL ISLAND
Dublin Bay
North East Dublin
www.northbullisland.com

Bull Island might not look like much to its extremely flat terrain, but it's a beautiful spot for a walk. It's a bird spotters' paradise, and it's also very common to see Irish hares, harbour seals and grey seals on a good day. The island is accessible by way of the wooden bridge connected to the North Bull Wall.

284 LAMBAY ISLAND
Skerries
North East Dublin
www.skerriesseatours.ie/
trips.html

Four kilometres from the mainland of Portrane, this 250-hectare island is a natural breeding ground for all sorts of wildlife including grey seals, fallow deer, puffins, gulls and geese. Quite incredibly, you'll also find a small number of exotic red-necked wallabies here.

285 IRELAND'S EYE
Howth
North East Dublin
www.islandferries.net

From the East Pier in Howth a boat will take you on a 15-minute journey to Ireland's Eye. This rugged looking 22-hectare uninhabited island is a bird sanctuary. It's also a safe spot to swim and it has a sandy beach for those wishing to relax. There's also the ruins of a church dating back to 700 AD and a Martello tower from the 19th century.

281 DALKEY ISLAND

5
LANES
to love

---

286 JOHNSON'S COURT
Off Grafton St
St Stephen's Green &
Grafton St ②

This lane links Grafton Street to Clarendon Street. It's not very long nor very wide but it's usually lit up with overhanging fairy lights and looks fantastic. Once the home of HMV's flagship music store in Dublin, now you can find jewellery stores here, as well as St Teresa's Church and occasional buskers.

287 MERCHANT'S ARCH
Temple Bar ③

This rather short lane leads from the heart of Temple Bar out onto the quays. It's peppered with interesting shops, including the fantastic South American Shop, China Blue (shoes), Hanley's Cornish Pasties and the superb Mexican eatery El Grito.

288 CRAMPTON COURT
Off Dame St
Trinity College &
Old City ①

Coming from either end, this is a rather unassuming looking lane, but coming at it from the Dame Street direction, it actually opens out into a colourful courtyard, then continues onto a lovely lane full of wall art before turning into a hanging wall garden. Surprise after surprise.

289 UPPER DAME LANE

From Trinity St
Trinity College &
Old City ③

This first half of Dame Lane is extremely popular for nights out. On the one side you have the back end and smoking sections of The Bankers Bar, Sweeney's and the Mercantile. On the opposite side you have 4 Dame Lane, The Stag's Head and The Dame Tavern. It's a particularly vibrant area of the city with musicians performing out on the street.

290 LOWER DAME LANE

From Great George's St
Trinity College &
Old City ③

As night comes and the lights turn on this continuation of Dame Street looks great, with all the brickwork on the left and a Kathmandu Kitchen on the right. If you keep walking to the end you'll reach the gates of Dublin Castle and Chez Max. This lane is also a handy shortcut away from the throngs on Dame Street.

286 JOHNSON'S COURT

5 marvellous
MURALS and ART WALLS

---

291 THE TARA BUILDING

Tara St
O'Connell Street &
the Quays ④
www.thetarabuilding.com
www.maserart.com

This place has been given a new purpose as a co-working and creative space. It's a hub for ambitious professionals, offering workshops and classes. Stand outside and gaze at incredibly colourful wall art by Dublin artist Maser; it has transformed the entire area.

292 JAMES EARLY'S JOYCEAN MASTERPIECE

AT: BLOOMS HOTEL
6 Anglesea St
Temple Bar ③
www.blooms.ie

James Earley's work on the Blooms Hotel is absolutely stunning. It's well worth a stop to appreciate. Many of the characters from Joyce's *Ulysses* are spray-painted larger than life on each side of the hotel. Rather than looking tacky, it's an examplary display of talent.

293 TÁIN OR SETANTA MOSAIC MURAL

Behind Eason
off Nassau St
Trinity College &
Old City ①

The life of the Irish hero Cuchulainn is displayed in all its glory with this unique and somewhat hidden mural, made by Desmond Kinney 43 years ago. The Setanta (or Táin) Wall also depicts that great Irish epic *The Cattle Raid of Cooley*, when our hero defended Ulster from invading forces set on stealing the Brown Bull of Cooley.

294 STORMZY

Smithfield Square
Smithfield &
Stoneybatter ⑥

This huge tribute to UK grime artist Stormzy popped up overnight. The work was done by a crew calling themselves Subset and is based on a scene from the music video *Shut up*. It's a classy piece of work and is a fitting sign of the times. Stormzy has had a huge year topping the charts with his debut album.

295 BP FALLON

AT: BUTTON FACTORY
Curved St
Temple Bar ③

A commemoration from one Dublin hero – artist Maser – to another – BP Fallon. Though he is living in the USA now, Fallon was an unmistakable Dublin character, well known for his bowler hat. He was a jack-of-all-trades (a broadcaster, journalist, musician, photographer and DJ) and worked with various influential figures over the years like Led Zeppelin, U2 and My Bloody Valentine.

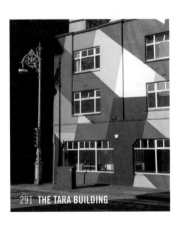

291 THE TARA BUILDING

The 5 annual

CELEBRATIONS

not to miss

---

296 DUBLIN INTERNATIONAL FILM FESTIVAL
February
www.diff.ie

It might not be as prolific as Cannes or Berlin but the Dublin Film Festival has a lot to offer for the cinephile. Its scale and ambition have grown over the past 15 years screening world premieres of local and international talent across a multitude of locations, and attracting a number of guest celebrities from Al Pacino to Kristin Scott Thomas.

297 BLOOMSDAY FESTIVAL
June
www.bloomsdayfestival.ie

Another a celebration of the great Dublin writer James Joyce. The Festival commemorates and relives his greatest achievement, the novel *Ulysses*, which takes place entirely on one day, the 16th of June 1904. Named after central character Leopold Bloom, the Festival encompasses several events, from literary tours to pub-crawls and from discussions and readings to performances.

298 DUBLIN LBTGQ PRIDE

June
www.dublinpride.ie

A celebration of all things LGBTQ, Dublin Pride is a reminder of the sizeable change that has taken place in this city over the last few years. There are a number of events and live music performances, at the centre of which is the Dublin Pride Parade usually followed by post parade celebrations around Merrion Square.

299 OKTOBERFEST

September/October
Dublin Docklands
O'Connell Street &
the Quays ④
www.oktoberfest-dublin.de

The German celebration of beer and traditional cuisine takes over the Docklands each year bringing with it Bavarian bands, German DJs and women in traditional dirndl serving proper steins of Erdinger. Do break German habits and try the Danish hotdogs. Try to get there early, as seats and space are limited.

300 INTERNATIONAL LITERATURE FESTIVAL

May
www.ilfdublin.com

An annual gathering to celebrate all things prose and poetry, with readings, interviews, signings and debate. Every year serious literary talent, both local and international, comes to Dublin to engage with readers and fans alike. There is something for everyone here, with all genres and preferences catered for.

5 alternative
CITY TOURS

301 GLASNEVIN CEMETERY MUSEUM

Finglas Road,
Glasnevin
North Dublin ⑧
+353 (0)1 882 6550
www.glasnevinmuseum.ie

A cemetery tour and museum may not be everyone's cup of tea but it is a unique and interesting experience. The museum is open every day and there are various guided tours around the cemetery twice daily. Depending on where your interests are you can book the 1916 tour, the literary tour, the military tour, the famous women of Glasnevin tour or many others.

302 GRAVEDIGGER GHOST BUS TOUR

STARTS AT: EXTREME IRELAND
TOURIST INFO
37 College Green
Trinity College &
Old City ①
+353 (0)85 102 3646
www.thegravedigger.ie

In the course of 2 ghoulish hours you will be taken aboard a dark black bus and transported back 600 years to listen to the tales and horrors of Dublin's past. Meanwhile your spectral guide points out relevant spots on the route. At the end a free refreshment awaits you at the Gravedigger's Pub – and also a surprise.

303 BRAM STOKER'S CASTLE DRACULA

Clontarf Road
North Dublin ⑧
+353 (0)1 851 2151
www.castledracula.ie

Though they may not have invented vampire fiction (see Le Fanu's *Carmilla*) the Irish make a rightful claim on Dracula. On this tour you will arrive at a hidden door and follow a tunnel underground to reach Castle Dracula, upon which you will be taken on a bloodcurdling tour by a litany of hosts, right into the master's lair.

304 DUBLIN LITERARY WALKING TOUR

www.dublinfree
walkingtour.ie/literature

Some of the greatest names in world literature have come from this small city: Joyce, Yeats, Wilde, Swift, Stoker, Beckett, Shaw, … This superb walking tour will take in all the great landmarks synonymous with these writers. In the course of 2,5 hours you'll see Yeats' Abbey Theatre, the home and statue of Oscar Wilde and many other remarkable sights.

305 RUTH RUA FASHION TOURS

www.ruaruth.com

Using a different location one Saturday each month from May to October, fashion stylist, writer and historian Ruth Rua leads private tours around Dublin exploring the secret style history of Dublin. Follow in the footsteps of our many furriers, dressmakers and manufacturers and visit a number of hidden landmarks and once famed shops and boutiques. Booking essential.

5 *stunning*
GARDENS

---

306 IVEAGH GARDENS

Clonmel St
St Stephen's Green &
Grafton St ②
+353 (0)1 475 7816
www.iveaghgardens.ie

During June and July the Iveagh Gardens host a number of concerts but for the greater part they are a stunning spot to go for a walk or relax and eat lunch. The gardens have over 300 years of history behind them, and they hold a maze, a rosarium, fountains and a cascade.

307 GARDEN OF REMEMBRANCE

Parnell Square East,
Rotunda
North Dublin ④
www.heritageireland.ie/
en/dublin/gardenof
remembrance

Dedicated to 'all those who gave their lives in the cause for Irish freedom', the Garden of Remembrance is a small but sombre tribute with an incredible sculpture by Oisin Kelly – based on the Irish legend of the *Children of Lir* – as its focal point. It is a garden for quiet reflection rather than picnics and music.

308 BLESSINGTON STREET BASIN

Blessington Street Park
North Dublin ④

Once a drinking-water reservoir, now a park, Blessington Street Basin is perhaps the most unusual park in Dublin as it is 80% water and 20% land (this includes the artificial duck/swan island and the beautiful reservoir lodge). It is an important slice of natural beauty at only a 10-minute walk from O'Connell Street.

309 IRISH NATIONAL WAR MEMORIAL GARDENS

Islandbridge
Kilmainham &
Liberties ⑤
*www.opwdublin
commemorative.ie/
war-memorial*

These gardens were designed by Sir Edwin Lutyens and laid out in the 1930s by ex-servicemen. They are made up of various sections, like the rose gardens bordered by the granite book rooms and the domed temple. The location adjacent an entrance of Phoenix Park is ideal, with a main road on one side parallel to the Liffey on the other.

310 ARDGILLAN CASTLE AND VICTORIAN GARDENS

Strifeland, Balbriggan
North Dublin ⑧
+353 (0)1 849 2212
www.ardgillancastle.ie

To be fair, this is not just a garden. It's a castle and demesne replete with a park, tea rooms and art exhibits, which makes for a good day trip. But the gardens are exquisite: the rose garden and conservatory, the walled garden (with a section for herbs, one for fruit and one for vegetables) and the four ornamental gardens.

308 BLESSINGTON STREET BASIN

5

NEIGHBOURHOODS

to investigate

---

311 STONEYBATTER
Smithfield &
Stoneybatter ⑥

After years of being known for all the wrong reasons, Stoneybatter began trending late 2015, early 2016. The Guardian published an article on the area and since then money and culture have poured in, and all kinds of pubs, cafes, eateries and shops (many of which are featured throughout this guide) have sprouted up.

312 DALKEY
South Dublin ⑨

Once a Viking settlement and an important port, now home to a number of sights like Dalkey Castle and a harbour with boats to take you to Dalkey Island. There are fantastic views and a lot of great food and drink options. Dalkey has also been home to Van Morrison and Maeve Binchy and still is home to Bono, The Edge and Neil Jordan.

313 PORTOBELLO

Ranelagh &
Rathmines ⑦

Portobello has long been a property hotspot. It's a very desirable city-suburb thanks to the combination of its proximity to canals, Camden Street pubs and various shops. Everything is within a short walking distance of one another, even the city centre is only a 10-minute walk away.

314 PHIBSBOROUGH

North Dublin ④

North of Stoneybatter/Smithfield and a 20-minute walk from O'Connell Street, Phibsborough has an abundance of places to check out. It's a very active, vibrant place with a mix of old and new venues. Sports bars and cafes sit comfortably next to the latest signs of gastro gentrification in the form of artisanal delis and shops.

315 CLONTARF

North Dublin ⑧

This north side coastal suburb overlooking Bull Island was the location for the famous Battle of Clontarf in 1014. Nowadays, it is home to a number of attractions including Dollymount Beach, St Anne's Park and Clontarf Castle. There are well-known watering holes and very good restaurants on Vernon Avenue and Clontarf Road.

312 **DALKEY**

316 ST STEPHEN'S GREEN

5

PARKS

to wander in

---

316 ST STEPHEN'S GREEN

St Stephen's Green &
Grafton St ②
www.ststephens
greenpark.ie

The epicentre of south Dublin city in many ways, it provides the perfect lunch benches and stretches of grass on warmer days, if you don't mind the noise and chaos that sometimes ensues. Duck and swan ponds, gardens and a playground are all steeped in 400 years of history, with various sculptures and monuments of interest dotted around.

317 BLACKROCK PARK

Blackrock
South Dublin ⑨
www.dlrcoco.ie/en/parks-
outdoors/parks/blackrock-
park

A very well-kept park right next to the sea, at the centre of which there are a pond and bird island, a playground and an outdoor workout area. There are great views here and a lot of space to wander around and its proximity to Blackrock Village makes a visit ideal for shopping or eating out.

318 **MARLAY PARK**

16 Grange Road,
Rathfarnham
South Dublin ⑨
+353 (0)1 205 4700
www.dlrcoco.ie/en/parks-outdoors/parks/marlay-park

This huge 121-hectare park has it all. In the summer months it hosts a number of huge concerts but there is much to love here all year round as well: beautiful forestry, woodlands and ponds as well as tennis courts, a golf course, football, GAA and cricket pitches, two children's playgrounds, craft shops, cafes and an operating miniature railway.

319 **ST ENDA'S PARK (WITH ITS HUDSON FOLLIES)**

Grange Road,
Rathfarnham
South Dublin ⑨
+353 (0)1 493 4208
www.pearsemuseum.ie

Home to the magnificent Patrick Pearse Museum and a number of intriguing landmarks like the Hudson Follies and the Hermit's Cave. There is a lot of history here, not just regarding Pearse, the leader of the 1916 Easter Rising, but also regarding the earlier Irish rebellion leader Robert Emmet and, amazingly, British army officer Sir Neville Chamberlain.

320 **ST ANNE'S PARK**

All Saints Road,
Raheny
North Dublin ⑧
www.clontarf.ie/history-of-clontarf/st-annes-park

It was Sir Arthur Guinness himself who planted the oaks and pines and pushed the development of St Anne's Park. These days the park is home to a rose festival, a farmers' market, Victorian stables, follies, a walled garden, woodlands and a spectacular tree sculpture by Tommy Craggs, in the northeast corner.

5 places to visit in
PHOENIX PARK

North Dublin ⑧
+353 (0)87 228 9698 (Park Rangers)
+353 (0)1 820 5800 (info)
www.phoenixpark.ie

321 DUBLIN ZOO
+353 (0)1 474 8900
www.dublinzoo.ie

The 28-hectare Dublin Zoo originally opened its doors in 1831. A lot has changed for the better since then and the zoo now boasts an African savannah, seal shows, feeding times, a house of reptiles, a South American house, Asian forests and a variety of places to eat and drink for all the family.

322 ÁRAS AN UACHTARÁIN
www.president.ie

Built in 1751, this is known as the home of Irish President Michael D. Higgins and his wife Sabina. Many dignitaries from all over the world have been welcomed here, including Pope John Paul II, Nelson Mandela, Queen Elizabeth II, Presidents Kennedy and Obama. There are guided tours of the building and the vast gardens.

323 PAPAL CROSS

www.phoenixpark.ie/
about/sightsofthepark

This 35-metre steel cross was erected for the visit of Pope John Paul II in 1979, and constructed by John Sisk & Sons. On the day of his arrival in Phoenix Park, on 29th September, the pope spoke to a crowd of some 1,25 million people. When he died, thousands gathered here leaving flowers.

324 VISITOR CENTRE

www.phoenixpark.ie/
visitorcentre

The Visitor Centre offers a free self-guided tour into the history of Phoenix Park. Visitors can enjoy the exhibition rooms and presentations as well as the adjoining Ashtown Castle and Gardens. There is also a restaurant and cafe with outdoor courtyard seating. Children's workshops take place on Sunday mornings.

325 PICNICKING ALONGSIDE FALLOW DEER

www.phoenixparkbook.
com/deer.htm

The Phoenix Park deer are fairly skittish animals and mostly part they like to stay together in a pack and keep to themselves. Feeding them isn't really advised but you can bring your own picnic and use one of the many allotted tables to eat while enjoying the presence of the animals.

5 important places in the
H I S T O R Y
of Dublin

---

326 **THE CROPPIES ACRE**

7 Benburb St,
Arran Quay
Smithfield &
Stoneybatter ⑥
+353 (0)1 702 8811
www.heritageireland.ie/
en/dublin/thecroppiesacre

In front of Collins Barracks you can admire this memorial to the Croppy Boys (a name given to them because of their cropped hairstyles) who fought in the 1798 rebellion. It is believed that this was their final resting place after their executions. It is also the home to Eamonn O'Doherty's Anna Livia sculpture.

327 **FUSILIERS' MEMORIAL ARCH**

Main entrance to
St Stephen's Green
St Stephen's Green &
Grafton St ②

This must be one of the most familiar Dublin landmarks. It was erected in 1907 and commemorates the Royal Dublin Fusiliers who fought (on both sides) and died during the Second Boer War (1899-1902). As you look towards it, note the faded bullet markings from the Easter Rising and as you walk under it, notice the lists of names on the underside of the arch.

328 ARBOUR HILL CEMETERY

Arbour Hill
Smithfield &
Stoneybatter ⑥
+353 (0)1 821 3021
www.heritageireland.ie/
en/dublin/arbourhillce-
metery

This cemetery is one of the most haunting and meditative spots in Dublin. It's the resting place for 14 of the last 1916 leaders, taken from Kilmainham Gaol (prison) after their execution. Clipped grass and flat slabs of granite lead up to a wide inscribed limestone wall, with another set of graves across from it, against the prison wall.

329 HEIRLOOMS & HAND-ME-DOWNS

The Liberties
Kilmainham &
Liberties ⑤
www.chrisreidartist.com/
heirlooms_plaques.html

In 2009 artist Chris Reid created 21 unique bronze plaques to place all around the The Liberties neighbourhood. Each inscription is based on actual recordings made by locals between 2004-2008. It's a great idea and, for those who are interested, it allows you some insight into how lives were once lived in this area. There is a map on the website.

330 MAGAZINE FORT

Phoenix Park
North Dublin ⑧
+353 (0)1 677 0095

In winter, there are free guided tours around what remains of this Magazine Fort. Once occupied by the British Armed Forces, it became an ammunition store for the Irish Defense Forces after the Anglo-Irish Treaty in 1922. It has a unique star-like structure with look-out towers at the corners.

5 perfect
COASTAL SPOTS
with a view

---

331 HIGH ROCK

Coast Road, Malahide
North Dublin ⑧
www.enjoymalahide.com/
home/beach/high-rock

Walking over the dark jagged rocks on either side feels like walking on a long concrete plank amidst the crashing of waves, but the stunning view across the Irish Sea on a good day is undeniable. High Rock is a popular place to swim, but don't try to unless you're a competent swimmer, as the currents can be quite strong.

332 DÚN LAOGHAIRE PIERS

East and West Pier,
Dún Laoghaire
South Dublin ⑨
www.dunlaoghaire.ie/ttd/
dun-laoghaire-pier

The East Pier is the more popular of these two piers, especially on Sundays when the world seems to go for a walk. The space in between the piers is filled with an assortment of boats. The views are spectacular from both piers but if you like solitude, choose the West Pier.

333 THE GREAT SOUTH WALL

Ringsend
South Dublin ⑨

The Great South Wall remains one of the longest sea walls in all of Europe. It runs for 4 kilometres from Poolbeg out into Dublin Bay. The path is wide enough, so don't be scared of being swept away.

334 KILLINEY OBELISK

Killiney Hill,
Scalpwilliam
South Dublin ⑨

If you can find a parking-place and wrangle your way through the dog walkers and the brambles, take on the steep path and push yourself up to the peak: this is a very rewarding walk. At the top, towering above everything else, is a simple Obelisk erected in 1792. The views are incomparable: Bray Head, Wicklow Mountains and even Wales on a good clear day.

335 THE NOSE OF HOWTH

Howth Head,
Howth Village
North Dublin ⑧

The Nose of Howth makes for a nice coastal walk with your choice of views, including Lambay Island and Ireland's Eye. There's also a burial cairn and the unmistakable Baily Lighthouse. This is a fine spot for taking in some fresh salty sea air, but take care as parts of the path are extremely close to the cliff edge.

334 KILLINEY OBELISK

335 THE NOSE OF HOWTH

5 special
LIBRARIES and
ARCHIVES

---

336 THE OLD LIBRARY
AT: TRINITY COLLEGE
College Green
Trinity College &
Old City ①
+353 (0)1 896 1000
www.tcd.ie/library/
old-library

Some of you may know that the Old Library is home to the famous Book of Kells, a 9th-century Gospel manuscript. The main chamber of the Old Library is called the Long Room; it is home to over 200.000 of the oldest books, which makes this one of the most impressive libraries in the world.

337 NATIONAL LIBRARY OF IRELAND
Kildare St
St Stephen's Green &
Grafton St ②
+353 (0)1 603 0200
www.nli.ie

A sacred place for all book lovers and writers alike, the National Library of Ireland houses, amongst other things, the personal notes of Seamus Heaney, Roddy Doyle, James Joyce and their likes. In fact, it holds the most comprehensive collection of Irish history and writing, providing immaculate preservation of all manuscripts.

338 NATIONAL PHOTO-GRAPHIC ARCHIVE
Meeting House Square
Temple Bar ③
+353 (0)1 603 0373
www.nli.ie/en/national-
photographic-archive.aspx

The NPA, opened in 1998, is located in Temple Bar. It is home to over 20.000 glass plate negatives from between 1870 and 1954 that have been digitised. They are available for viewing online or by appointment. There is also a reading room.

339 MARSH'S LIBRARY

St Patrick's Close
Wood Quay
Kilmainham &
Liberties ⑤
+353 (0)1 454 3511
www.marshlibrary.ie

This is probably Dublin's most eerie, Harry Potter-esque library. Founded in the 18th century and thus an example of the late Renaissance/early Enlightenment period, it's still in use today. There are dozens of beautiful dark oak bookcases here and cages to read in privacy. There's even a skull in one, where one poor chap never got out.

340 MILITARY ARCHIVES

Cathal Brugha Barracks
Military Road
Ranelagh &
Rathmines ⑦
+353 (0)1 804 6457
*www.militaryarchives.ie/
en/home*

This is the place to go for all things on military record. With a huge database, there are dozens of collections of preserved historical documents. Many of them, such as the Air Corps Museums Collection, the Civil War Captured Documents and Emergency Defense Plans, can be viewed from special reading rooms. Appointment necessary.

339 MARSH'S LIBRARY

5 places dedicated to
JAMES JOYCE

341 **JAMES JOYCE STATUE**
2 Earl St North
O'Connell Street &
the Quays ④

Balancing with his walking stick, one leg wrapped around the other, hat tilted, it's possible that our famous author James Joyce never looked so dapper as he does here in North Earl Street. Installed by Marjorie Fitzgibbon in 1990, the statue has been given the common nickname of 'the prick with the stick.'

342 **JAMES JOYCE CENTRE**
35 Great George's St
North
North Dublin ④
+353 (0)1 878 8547
www.jamesjoyce.ie

Saved from demolition and funded by a number of private investors, the James Joyce Centre was opened in 1996. Furniture was provided by Paul Léon, Joyce's friend and secretary, with whom he stayed while writing pieces of *Finnegan's Wake*. There's a Joyce study, a death mask, three documentary films on show, and also the original door of Leopold Bloom's house.

343 SWENY'S JOYCEAN PHARMACY

1 Lincoln Place
Trinity College &
Old City ①
+353 (0)87 713 2157
www.sweny.ie/site

This famous pharmacy is mentioned in *Ulysses*; in fact there is a lengthy description of Sweny's in the book, which ends with the protagonist purchasing a lemony bar of soap and drifting out across the city. Sweny's has been preserved as it was in Joyce's time, with walls of bottles, jars and potions. It is run by volunteers.

344 JAMES JOYCE TOWER & MUSEUM

Sandycove Point
Sandycove
South Dublin ⑨
+353 (0)85 198 2218
www.joycetower.ie

This free admission attraction in the village of Sandycove is open daily. It is another example of the Martello towers that the British built all along the coast at various points to protect against a French invasion. Inside, it houses the James Joyce Museum, which boasts some very rare memorabilia.

345 JAMES JOYCE PLAQUE

Near Eason on the
pavement of Abbey St
O'Connell Street &
the Quays ④

In 1998, as part of the forthcoming Millennium celebrations, 14 plaques were set into the sidewalks so one could follow in the footsteps of Leopold Bloom, should they wish to do so. This one reads 'Aeolus – the offices of the Evening Telegraph (Ulysses, Episode 7)', and alludes to the character of Bloom visiting the offices of the Evening Telegraph in chapter 7 of Ulysses.

5 sites to visit in
KILMAINHAM &
THE LIBERTIES

346 IMMA

Royal Hospital, Military
Road, Kilmainham
+353 (0)1 612 9900
www.imma.ie

The vast IMMA was founded in 1864 as a Royal Hospital for retired soldiers and by 1991 it was open as the Irish Museum of Modern Art. The grounds and gardens are stunning and the exhibitions have hosted some of the biggest Irish and international names around including Duncan Campbell, Lucien Freud, Patrick Hennessy, Diego Rivera and Frida Kahlo.

347 ST PATRICK'S CATHEDRAL

St Patrick's Close,
Wood Quay
+353 (0)1 453 9472
www.stpatrickscathedral.ie

You don't need to be religious to appreciate the scale and presence of St Patrick's Cathedral, the National Cathedral of the Church of Ireland. It was built in 1191, and it's the largest and tallest church in Ireland, replete with wonderful stained glass windows. It's also the burial ground of *Gulliver's Travels* author Jonathan Swift.

348 THE HOUSE OF THE DEAD & DINNER

15 Usher's Island
+353 (0)86 054 8880

The House of the Dead on Usher's Island was the setting for James Joyce's most famous short story 'The Dead' from *Dubliners*; it's also a magnificent film by the way. The house can be rented out so you can dine on exactly what the protagonists of this story ate (by appointment only for groups of 10 to 14 people).

349 KILMAINHAM GAOL

Inchicore Road,
Kilmainham
+353 (0)1 453 5984
www.kilmainhamgaol museum.ie

This *gaol* (jail) is not only symbolic of Irish nationalist pride; it is also a pivotal connection between all the rebellions and conflicts that took place after the *gaol* was opened in 1796. There are two chapels (one for Catholics, one for Protestants) and two wings, and also a haunting stonebreakers yard where the 14 leaders of the 1916 Easter Rising were executed.

350 TEELING WHISKEY DISTILLERY

13-17 Newmarket,
Merchants Quay
North Dublin ⑧
+353 (0)1 531 0888
www.teelingdistillery.com

Once known as the 'Golden Triangle', The Liberties used to be the epicentre of whiskey distilling. Only open three years, the Teeling Whiskey Distillery is the newest one in over 100 years, and it was built on the remains of the old Walter Teeling distillery. There's no other distillery like it in Dublin. Open 7 days a week with tour guides and tastings.

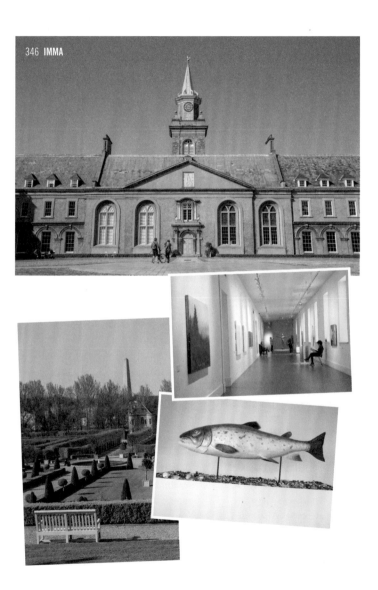

5

IMPORTANT STATUES

351 JAMES LARKIN
O'Connell St Lower
O'Connell Street &
the Quays ④

James Larkin was the founder of
the Workers' Union of Ireland and a
socialist activist. He was known for his
involvement in a number of industrial
disputes between workers and employers,
in particular the Dublin Lockout of 1913.
His statue really stands out as one of the
most emphatic and expressive of all the
statues scattered around Dublin.

352 CIRCLE OF MERCY
Baggot St Lower
St Stephen's Green &
Grafton St ②

Outside the Mercy International Centre is
the statue of Catherine Elizabeth McAuley,
the founder of the Sisters of Mercy, a
charitable cause dedicated to working
with and helping the poor. The statue was
designed by Michael Burke in 1994.

353 THE VICTIMS
Merrion Square Park
St Stephen's Green &
Grafton St ②

A wonderful macabre work by Andrew
O'Connor, The Victim is a dead soldier
lying between two standing figures: The
Mother of the Hero and The Wife (or The
Mother of Sorrows). The statue originated
as a part of an unexecuted project for a
war memorial for Washington, DC.

354 WOLFE TONE

Wolfe Tone, revolutionary leader, founding member of the United Irishmen and overall republican standard-bearer, has his own statue and square, tucked into a corner of St Stephen's Green. The statue is the work of Irish sculptor Edward Delaney and was erected in 1967.

355 THE JOKER'S CHAIR

Perhaps not as weighty or historical as others on this list, nevertheless the Joker's Chair is a memorial to one of Ireland's greatest TV actors and most beloved satirical comedians, Dermot Morgan. He reached the peak of his success as the character of Father Ted in the series of the same name. Morgan died of a died of a heart attack at the age of 45.

353 THE VICTIMS

5 Rowan Gillespie
SCULPTURES

www.rowangillespie.com

356 FAMINE

Custom House Quay
O'Connell Street &
the Quays ④

These six harrowing figures, emaciated and barely alive, are depicted emigrating from Ireland during the Great Famine (1845-1852). Approximately one million people died then. On an opposing shore in Toronto (where some 40.000 Irish landed), Rowan's bronze figures can be seen rejoicing at Ireland Park, the journey a success.

357 JUDGEMENT

AT: SUTHERLAND SCHOOL OF
LAW (UCD)
Belfield
South Dublin ⑨

Rowan Gillespie is a world-renowned sculptor but this is perhaps one of his lesser-known pieces. It shows two tall slim men with long beards, standing face-to-face in Roman attire, one pointing at the other. Both look deep in conversation. Apparently *Judgement* is in response to a philosophical debate on Iraq at the time.

358 BIRDY
AT: CRESCENT HALL
Mount St
St Stephen's Green &
Grafton St ②

Hunkered on a windowsill over the door of Crescent Hall, is this intriguing little character called *Birdy*. Slightly reminiscent of the titular character of Birdy in Alan Parker's film by her crouched stance, she actually represents freedom: a bird or woman freed from her cage and ready to take flight.

359 ASPIRATION
AT: TREASURY BUILDING
Grand Canal St
Trinity College &
Old City ①

Certainly one of the more unusual statues in Dublin, *Aspiration* shows Gillespie's bronze figure climbing the side of the Treasury Building, one hand ahead of the other, his/her head turned to the side. Originally it was a male climber but protests from local businessmen lead to a change in the anatomy.

360 PROCLAMATION
Inchicore Road
Kilmainham &
Liberties ⑤

Standing across the street from Kilmainham Gaol stands this perhaps odd-looking abstract sculpture to commemorate those that fought and died in the 1916 Easter Rising. Wiry limbless figures stand in a circle around a table with the proclamation, each blindfolded. Each has the verdict and sentence stamped on them and is marked by bullet holes.

5
HARRY CLARKES
to find

---

www.harryclarke.net

361 ST PETER AND ST PAUL
Church of Ireland, Sandford Road, Ranelagh
Ranelagh & Rathmines ⑦

Harry Clarke was a hugely acclaimed Irish illustrator and a master stained-glass artist. You can admire his work all over the city if you know where to look. This Art Deco-style piece was commissioned almost 100 years ago and depicts the Saints Peter and Paul alongside each other in their own windows. Each has a smaller lower panel relating to their back stories.

362 SAINTS HUBERT, LUKE AND GEORGE
St Brigid's Church of Ireland, Castleknock
North Dublin ⑧

This three-piece window has one section for each of the titular saints. St George is depicted in all three windows doing a number of things, including rescuing a poor maiden from a dragon. St Hubert takes centre stage in the second window meeting a stag. The rest is all St Luke, physician and painter of the Virgin Mary.

363 ANGEL OF PEACE AND HOPE

Holy Trinity Church, Killiney

South Dublin ⑨

A commemorative war memorial (1915) from a father to a son who was killed in the First World War, this is one large singular window. The Angel is depicted from the side with red hair and a halo. Again there is a dove present and also the family's coat of arms is shown.

364 THE ANNUNCIATION AND THE CORONATION OF THE VIRGIN IN GLORY

St Joseph's Church, Terenure

South Dublin ⑨

The Annunciation celebrates the announcement that the Virgin Mary is going to conceive. The Holy Spirit is present in the form of a dove. On the right hand side is *The Coronation of the Virgin in Glory* (1923). Mary is seen here being crowned, omitting, what could be, tongues of flame. The window was signed by Clarke himself at the very bottom on the left.

365 THE SACRED HEART, ST MARGARET AND ST JOHN EUDES

Vincentian Fathers Church of St Peter, Phibsborough

North Dublin ⑧

There is a lot going on here in this wonderful and detailed three-piece window from 1919. Saint Margaret Mary, her Sacred Heart and Jesus himself are present throughout (Jesus on the cross, Jesus doing his duties, the risen Lord). St Patrick is in there too, shamrock at hand. And of course, as the title denotes, you can find St John, who was the founder of the Society of the Priests of Jesus and Mary.

KERLIN GALLERY

45 PLACES
TO ENJOY CULTURE

———

5 *must-see*
DUBLIN ART GALLERIES

─────────

366 KERLIN GALLERY

Anne's Lane, South
Anne Street
St Stephen's Green &
Grafton St ②
+353 (0)1 670 9093
www.kerlingallery.com

Dublin may not have the money and pulling power of New York, Paris or London but there are still some intimate and beautifully curated contemporary art galleries worth seeking out. The exhibitions calendar of Kerlin is very rich and culturally diverse, featuring the abstract, the colourful, the beautiful, the bold and the bizarre.

367 MOLESWORTH GALLERY

16 Molesworth St
St Stephen's Green &
Grafton St ②
+353 (0)1 679 1548
*www.molesworth
gallery.com*

Much like the Kerlin Gallery, the Molesworth Gallery is a very exciting space. It is constantly challenging visitors to rethink how they look at art and interact with it, as recent exhibitions by Michael Beirne, Martin Redmond and Helen Blake can attest to. There are eight solo and two curated group exhibitions here annually.

368 DOUGLAS HYDE GALLERY

Trinity College
Trinity College &
Old City ①
+353 (0)1 896 1116
www.douglashyde
gallery.com

The Douglas Hyde Gallery was named after the first president of Ireland and usually hosts two artists at any one time; the bigger name in the large open Gallery 1 and another smaller exhibit in Gallery 2 (outsider art, photography, textiles). There's also a number of publications on sale.

369 TEMPLE BAR GALLERY + STUDIOS

5-9 Temple Bar
Temple Bar ③
+353 (0)1 671 0073
www.templebar
gallery.com

Featuring installations and performance art as well as sculpture and video, the Temple Bar Gallery works hand in hand with Artists Studios. It's a really interesting and engaging concept and it puts you right into the heart of the artist's community here in Dublin. Past exhibitions included Declan Clarke, Amie Siegel and Barbara Knezevic.

370 GREEN ON RED GALLERY

Park Lane
Spencer Dock
O'Connell Street &
the Quays ④
+353 (0)87 245 4282
www.greenonred
gallery.com

It's small but it manages to entertain both the Irish and international contemporary scene with 10 to 11 solo exhibitions a year and 1 to 2 group exhibitions. Many of the exhibitors also showcase abroad. Admire the starkly beautiful art carefully displayed around the white washed interior. The gallery offers a consultancy service for private collectors and businesses.

5 gems of the
HUGH LANE GALLERY

AT: CHARLEMONT HOUSE
Parnell Square North
North Dublin ④
+353 (0)1 222 5550
www.hughlane.ie

371 FRANCIS BACON STUDIO

Bacon's studio is as chaotic as his life was. Born in Dublin in 1909, he spent much of his life in Soho London drinking, gambling and painting his own unique brand of dark twisted surrealism/ expressionism. His paintings are some of the world's most expensive ones. In the Hugh Lane Gallery, his studio has been meticulously relocated for viewing.

372 SEAN SCULLY GALLERY

Like Bacon, Sean Sculley was born in Dublin and raised in London. In later years he settled in New York. Known as both a painter and a printmaker, his art is collected all over the world. This permanent exhibition provides a great insight into his world of abstract art.

271 FRANCIS BACON STUDIO

373 LOUIS LE BROCQUY

Before he passed away in 2012, le Brocquy had spent 70 odd years in the art world, his work and influence spanning across the globe with exhibitions just about everywhere. He was a man of many mediums but he was best remembered for his haunting *Portrait Heads*, on show here.

374 FRANK O'MEARA AND IRISH ARTISTS ABROAD

Split between Ireland and France, O'Meara died from malari at the age of 35. But in that brief time he was renowned for his evocative impressionist landscape painting. Alongside O'Meara's work, this collection presents other works by similar artists who also left Ireland to develop their styles.

375 RETURN OF THE HUGH LANE PICTURES
FROM NATIONAL GALLERY LONDON

Four priceless masterpieces have returned to Dublin after being on show in London: one by Renoir, one by Morisot (both impressionist masters), one buy early impressionist and realist Edouard Manet,and one by post-impressionist Camille Pisarro.

The best 5 venues to hear
MUSIC

---

376 THE SUGAR CLUB

8 Leeson St Lower
St Stephen's Green &
Grafton St ②
+353 (0)1 678 7188
www.thesugarclub.com

The Sugar Club is perhaps one of the most unique clubs in Dublin as it welcomes a very eclectic range of artists. Best known for its hip-hop, funk and jazz, it also hosts screenings of classic films and cult favourites. With its wood-panelled walls and unique tiered seating, it is an exciting and important multi-purpose Arts Centre.

377 THE MEZZ

23-24 Eustace St
Temple Bar ③
+353 (0)1 670 7655
www.mezz.ie

Reminiscent of Berlin's dive bars, The Mezz is all about live rock, blues and alternative bands. The stage is on a level with the crowd only a few feet away, which creates a very special intimate and immersive atmosphere. Big names as well as new up-and-coming bands get the chance to show what they're made of.

378 WHELAN'S

25 Wexford St
St Stephen's Green &
Grafton St ②
+353 (0)1 478 0766
www.whelanslive.com

After 25 years, Whelan's has become an Irish institution at this point. The roster of artists is ever evolving with everything from trad to rock and metal being played. Kila, Hozier, Sleaford Mods, Jeff Buckley, Lee Scratch Perry, Nick Cave and the Arctic Monkeys have all played here. They also do comedy nights.

379 JJ SMYTHS

12 Aungier St
St Stephen's Green &
Grafton St ②
+353 (0)1 475 2565
www.jjsmyths.com

There's nothing very special about the ground floor bar. It's a good old-fashioned bar with a cosy atmosphere but what you really want is to go upstairs: this is the home of live blues and jazz. There's music on most nights of the week. Check the website for further details but most of the good stuff kicks off around 8.30 pm.

380 BUTTON FACTORY

Curved St
Temple Bar ③
+353 (0)1 670 9105
www.buttonfactory.ie

Right bang in the middle of Temple Bar, this is one for the younger generation, by and large. Tribute bands play here regularly but most of the appeal lies in the newer emerging alternative acts and DJs. After a lot of refurbishments over the years, it's a sleek looking and intimate venue with a good loud sound system.

5
SCREENS
worth a look

---

381 HAPPENINGS
(venue: It's a surprise)
www.happenings.ie

Happenings is all about taking advantage of public spaces and, hopefully, good weather. You can expect pop-up screenings, music or yoga. Anytime. Anywhere. The best way to keep in the loop is to register on their website or through Facebook. Spontaneity is key and you will be informed of the event 48 hours beforehand.

382 IRISH FILM INSTITUTE
6 Eustace St
Temple Bar ③
+353 (0)1 679 3477
www.ifi.ie

The Irish Film Institute veers away from the multiplex popcorn and superhero films and instead presents the best of Irish and world cinema. You'll see some of the best films and premieres here that you won't see anywhere else in Dublin. There are also many festivals, workshops and special events throughout the year. Their shop is excellent for DVDs.

393 YE OLDE HURDY GURDY MUSEUM OF VINTAGE RADIO

6 Balscadden Road, Howth
North Dublin ⑧
www.hurdygurdyradio museum.wordpress.com

A hurdy-gurdy is a string instrument that omits sound once cranked, and can conjure melodies when played properly. It was also slang for a radio and so this museum is concerned with all things communication and so this museum, tucked away in a Martello Tower, is concerned with all things communication. Curator Pat Herbert is happy to show you around his collection of radios, gramophones and other paraphernalia.

394 THE MUSEUM FLAT AKA NELLIE'S FLAT

AT: THE IVEAGH TRUST
3-B Patrick St
Kilmainham &
Liberties ⑤
+353 (0)1 454 2312
www.theiveaghtrust.ie

Beginning in 1904, this flat saw many occupants, but when the Molloy family settled in by 1915, it was theirs for two generations. After the death of Nellie Molloy in 2002 it was decided, with the help of the Iveagh Trust, that the flat would be kept as a museum. It's a portal back in time and open for viewings Monday to Friday by appointment through the website.

395 THE LITTLE MUSEUM OF DUBLIN

15 St Stephen's Green
St Stephen's Green &
Grafton St ②
+353 (0)1 661 1000
www.littlemuseum.ie

Known as the people's museum of Dublin and situated in an 18th-century Georgian home, everything on show here has been donated by Dubliners over the years. The collection documents the history and timeline of the city itself. There are permanent and temporary exhibits. Visitation is by guided tour only and it's very popular, so book ahead.

395 THE LITTLE MUSEUM OF DUBLIN

5 *important and interesting*
THEATRES

---

396 THE ABBEY THEATRE
26-27 Abbey St Lower
O'Connell Street &
the Quays ④
+353 (0)1 878 7222
www.abbeytheatre.ie

The Abbey is synonymous with diversity and innovation, always showcasing an interesting mix of both local and international writers and artists. Founded in 1904 by W.B. Yeats and Lady Augusta Gregory, the Abbey has premiered classic works by J.M. Synge and Sean O'Casey as well as more contemporary classics from the likes of Sebastian Barry, Sam Shepard and Brian Friel.

397 THE GAIETY THEATRE
King St South
St Stephen's Green &
Grafton St ②
+353 (0)1 456 9569
www.gaietytheatre.ie

A little less of the dramatics here; and more musicals, comedy and pantomime. Opened in 1871, this theatre has been home to well-known shows like *Riverdance*, *Beauty and the Beast* and even the Eurovision Song Contest. The bronze handprints on the pavement outside include those of Luciano Pavarotti, Brendan Grace, Twink and John B. Keane.

398 SMOCK ALLEY THEATRE

6-7 Exchange St Lower
Temple Bar ③
+353 (0)1 677 0014
www.smockalley.com

After 350 years, The Smock Alley theatre finally reopened in 2012 as a theatre once again. Now it's a hub of creativity and a home for opera, installations, comedy, for song, dance and for art. There's an intimate main space, the red-bricked Boys School church venue and a banquet hall for hire.

399 THE NEW THEATRE

43 Essex St East
Temple Bar ③
+353 (0)1 670 3361
www.thenewtheatre.com

Slotted in at one end of Temple Bar just past all the Irish bars, Essex Street has a number of points of interest. And here, committed to giving artists, writers and performers a voice, The New Theatre has always had an interesting programme of films, plays and talks. It especially welcomes first time writers and performers and helps nurture their talent.

400 NUMBER TWENTY TWO

22 Anne St South
St Stephen's Green &
Grafton St ②
+353 (0)1 707 9899
www.numbertwentytwo.ie

An address of mystery. Behind the blue door however is an exclusive venue with much to show you. How about the wild and wonderful masked Masquerade and Spectacle? Or a cabaret night with circus and burlesque performers? Or a glamorous Cafe Society night? There are dinner and a show options and there's a stunning library bar. Check out the website and book ahead.

5
ARTISTS
worth investigating

---

401 ROBERT BALLAGH

Robert Ballagh is a very distinct artist. Influenced by pop art, his work is full of thick black lines and blocks of bright colour. His almost photorealistic portraits aside, Ballagh's work is often thematically political or historical, moving between abstract form and figurative painting of well-known figures or events.

402 DUNCAN CAMPBELL

Born in Dublin but based in Glasgow, Campbell was the 2014 recipient of the Turner Prize for his 54-minute short film *It for Others*. It's about, amongst other things, Marxist ideology, dance and African art. Much of his work focuses on a particular moment in history and he uses archival material to flesh out his projects. His 2009 film *Make It New, John* is an absolute must see.

403 MAINIE JELLETT

Jellett was an incredible trendsetter in the art world in the 1920s with her particular mix of abstract and cubist paintings. The development of her style was influenced by the art she saw while moving between Dublin, London and Paris. Her famous *Decoration* (1923) was one of the first abstract paintings shown in Ireland.

404 JACK BUTLER YEATS

J.B. Yeats (brother to W.B. Yeats) wasn't born here, but died here. He was an illustrator before becoming a painter working with oils and focusing on landscapes and figures. The way he thickly layered the colours to the canvas became a trademark. He moved between expressionism and symbolism depicting urban and rural Ireland.

405 SARAH PURSER

Purser was a famed stained glass artist as well as a brilliant portraitist, who studied in Switzerland, Ireland and France. Her talent lay in the understanding and use of complementary colour schemes and the rendering of realistic facial expressions of those who posed for her. She was in high demand and received many commissions from the British aristocracy.

5
WORDSMITHS
to discover

---

406 SHERIDAN LE FANU

One could say before Bram Stoker and his Dracula there was Sheridan Le Fanu. And rightly so. A master writer of the macabre, his ghost stories were hugely popular in Victorian times and his vampiric novella *Carmilla* predates Dracula by 26 years. His short story collections are an absolute must-read for anyone interested in gothic horror.

407 DERMOT BOLGER

A novelist, poet and playwright born and bred in Dublin, but based in Glasgow, Bolger has forged a long career from his writings about the working classes and the struggle of the individual in society. There's an unmistakable Irishness to his writing but he does cast his net out by removing us from the usual John McGahern/Frank McCourt Irish misery and into the modern world of Dublin, London and beyond.

408 ELIZABETH BOWEN

Bowen had an incredibly colourful private and social life; she often found herself brushing shoulders with the Bloomsbury Group, Carson McCullers, A.S. Byatt and Iris Murdoch, while in and out of affairs with men and women. But most importantly of all, there are her highly acclaimed novels: *The House in Paris*, *The Death of the Heart* and the Man Booker shortlisted *Eva Trout*.

409 EAVAN BOLAND

Most Irish people of a certain generation will have a recollection of Bolan's evocative and visually striking poems from their school days (*The Pomegranate* for instance). The writings of this multitalented poet, author and professor, focus mainly on the Irish identity and the position of women in today's society. She has won many awards and honours.

410 OLIVER ST JOHN GOGARTY

No, we're not talking about the overly expensive pub in Temple Bar but about the actual man it's named after. He was a man of many talents: a poet, an author, a failed doctor, even an athlete. He published several plays, books of prose (try and get a copy of *As I Was Going Down Sackville Street*) and poetry. He was immortalised in good friend James Joyce's *Ulysses* as the character Buck Mulligan.

THE ARK

20 THINGS TO DO WITH CHILDREN

5 ideas to go on
ADVENTURES

---

411 AIRFIELD ESTATE

Overend Avenue,
Dundrum
South Dublin ⑨
+353 (0)1 969 6666
www.airfield.ie

Established in 1974 for educational and recreational purposes, this 38-acre estate has everything you want for a full day of fun for children as well as adults. There's a cafe, a heritage museum and, most importantly, a farm and gardens. Children can explore and look for wild animals there, lend a helping hand milking the jersey cows or discover the rich fruit and vegetable gardens.

412 VIKING SPLASH TOUR

St Stephens Green North
St Stephen's Green &
Grafton St ②
+353 (0)1 707 6000
www.vikingsplash.com

On this unique little tour every participant gets to wear Viking headwear and is urged to howl out as the bus hurtles through the city with the lively guide pointing out historical landmarks. The highlight for most children is when the bus transforms into a boat and takes you onto the calm waters of Grand Canal Harbour.

413 FORT LUCAN OUTDOOR ADVENTURELAND

Westmanstown, Lucan
North Dublin ⑧
+353 (0)1 628 0166
www.fortlucan.com

Fort Lucan has it all. The central fort itself is built like a castle with a series of towers, ramparts and swing bridges connecting it all together. There are slides, there are drawbridges and much more. Fed up with this amazing playground? There's also go-karting, medieval crazy golf and two raging river waterslides.

414 RAINFOREST ADVENTURE GOLF

Dundrum Town Centre
South Dublin ⑨
+353 (0)1 296 4588
www.rainforest
adventuregolf.ie

What's better than golf? Adventure golf of course! And what's better than adventure golf? Rainforest adventure golf! Part educational, part silly and fun, this is a golf putting day out on which you make your way around the lands and temples of two ancient civilisations in the jungle, namely the Mayans and the Aztecs.

415 THE NATIONAL WAX MUSEUM PLUS

22-25 Westmoreland St
Trinity College &
Old City ①
+353 0(1) 671 8373
www.waxmuseumplus.ie

By the summer of 2017 the wax museum will have moved from its old home at Foster Place to a brand new location somewhere more central in the city. Children love the range of famous stars on show, the cartoon characters, aliens and Star Wars figures, and especially the more ghoulish and ghastly cast of famous freaks, vampires and monsters.

5 cool places to
LEARN AS YOU PLAY

---

416 THE ARK
11-A Eustace St
Temple Bar ③
+353 (0)1 670 7788
www.ark.ie

This cultural centre was built in 1995 to educate children about art and to help them discover and enjoy it however they wish. There are shows, painting lessons, watch-and-make classes and a lot of activities where children are immersed in art while being encouraged to get their hands dirty.

417 IMAGINOSITY - DUBLIN CHILDREN'S MUSEUM
Beacon South Quarter,
Sandyford
South Dublin ⑨
+353 (0)1 217 6130
www.imaginosity.ie

Imaginosity offers special exhibitions, activities and learning environments for all ages. There are spaces for babies and toddlers from 6 months to 3 years and there's a roof garden and three floors of play scenes and fun activities for children up to 9, including a village market, a garage, a library, a water lab, a puppet show and so much more.

418 PINE FOREST ART CENTRE
Glencullen, Kilternan
South Dublin ⑨
+353 (0)1 294 1220
www.pineforestartcentre.com

Pine Forest, an arts and crafts centre relatively high in the Dublin mountains, was founded in 1973 by artist and teacher Mary Carroll. There are all sorts of creative courses here that cover painting and sketching, the collecting of natural materials and forest trail talks and walks.

419 NATIONAL AQUATIC CENTRE

Snugborough Road,
Blanchardstown
North Dublin ⑧
+353 (0)1 646 4300
*www.national
aquaticcentre.ie*

Being one of Europe's largest indoor water centres, the National Aquatic Centre is a good place to learn how to swim. The highlight here is the Aquazone: a vast intricate twisting mesh of waterslides with names like Master Blaster, Green Giant Flume and Dark Hole Flume. Kids will also love the pirate ship.

420 DUBLINIA

Christ Church
St Michael's Hill,
Merchants Quay
Trinity College &
Old City ①
+353 (0)1 679 4611
www.dublinia.ie

Learning about Vikings and the Middle Ages couldn't be more fun than here. Kids can stand face-to-face with warriors of long ago, who fought bravely and lived a wild life of sword and steel. Discover what the city of Dublin looked like 700 years ago, marvel at all sorts of artefacts and visit St Michael's Tower.

416 THE ARK

420 DUBLINIA

5 ideal outdoor
PLAYGROUNDS

—

421 CABINTEELY PARK

Old Bray Road,
Cabinteely
South Dublin ⑨
+353 (0)1 205 4817

Dublin Council has spent a lot of time and money on improving and upgrading playgrounds and then building more of them across the city. The five in this list represent the scale and variety. The playground in Cabinteely Park stands out because it's so colourful and offers a wide range of constructs and because it's based in a good clean, safe environment.

422 DEERPARK

18 Mount Anville Road,
Mount Merrion
South Dublin ⑨
*www.mountmerrion.ie/
deerpark*

This beautiful 32-acre park, is family-friendly and open 24/7. It has a host of facilities that cater for dog walkers (there is an off-lease dog run area in the forest), joggers (a one mile exterior path and 5 exercise areas) and of course children – a huge playground lies in the northeast corner with towers, slides, swings and an ice-cream shop.

423 MARLAY PARK

(the bigger of the two)
16 Grange Road,
Rathfarnham
South Dublin ⑨
+353 (0)1 204 7244

This vast playground is immaculately maintained, and it has an assortment of weird and wonderful machines and equipment, some of them made from rope, others from wood. There are ramps and slides, swings, huge netted towers and so on. Once the kids run in here, it's hard to get them back out.

424 HERBERT PARK

4 Herbert Park,
Ballsbridge
South Dublin ⑨
+353 (0)1 660 1875

As in Marlay Park, there are two playgrounds here too. The smaller of the two, recently refurbished, is a nice play area for toddlers and slightly younger children. It has a soft wood chip floor and some very new but basic playthings; slide, fort, swings, spinning wheel, see-saw and climbing net.

425 FATHER COLLINS PARK

The Hole in The Wall
Road, Donaghmede
North Dublin ⑧
+353 (0)1 222 5278

Located in the middle of a 26-hectare park featuring running tracks, pitches, picnic areas and skate facilities, there are also two playgrounds. There is the typical range of imaginative slides and climbing equipment as well as the less familiar climbing bars, springers and a supernova (a difficult to master revolving wheel you must try to run with/on).

5 *for*
FOOD & SWEETS

426 THE CHOCOLATE WAREHOUSE
AT: MULCAHY KEANE INDUSTRIAL ESTATE
Greenhills Road, Walkinstown
South Dublin ⑨
+353 (0)1 450 0080
www.chocolate
warehouse.ie

The Chocolate Warehouse is behind some of the most delicious sugary treats like snowballs, tea cakes and macaroon bars, and is a fun place to take a tour or a workshop when you're entertaining kids, for example for a birthday party. The two-hour visit includes an educational video, a demonstration and then yes, the best bit: the hands-on session where you make your own chocolates from scratch.

427 SCRUMDIDDLY'S
4 Crofton Road, Dún Laoghaire
South Dublin ⑨
www.scrumdiddlys
world.com

Sugar overdose alert! Get your rocky road or apple crumble ice-cream, waffles or a crepe or just get your plain old boring vanilla ice-cream cone and cover it with Rolo's, Maltesers, jellies and lashings of chocolate sauce. It's entirely up to you.

428 CAPTAIN AMERICAS

44 Grafton St
St Stephen's Green &
Grafton St ②
+353 (0)1 671 5266
www.captainamericas.com

Chances are that kids will love this restaurant straight away, as it is named after a badass superhero. The interior is wall to wall with colourful memorabilia, so there's a lot to look at, and there is a special kids meal deal menu. Of course, the menu also has a lot to offer for adults, too. A very family-friendly place.

429 BAY RESTAURANT

367 Clontarf Road,
Clontarf
North Dublin ⑧
+353 (0)1 853 2406
www.bay.ie

Very friendly, very comfortable and in many ways perfect for the kids. Bring them on a Tuesday; they eat for free then. Bring them any other day and they can tackle smoothies and mini-burgers or small portions of spaghetti bolognese, cod or chicken. Ice creams and brownies for afters.

430 MILANOS

Crofton Road, Harbour
Square, Dun Laoghaire
South Dublin ⑨
+353 (0)1 663 7640
www.milano.ie

Milanos is always buzzing with hungry and eager kids. It's a firm favourite with young families, even those with fussy eaters, because who doesn't love pizza? Along with the puzzles and colouring pages on the menus, there are pizza making parties for the young – and the old – to bring an element of fun into the world of food from an early age.

THE GENERATOR HOSTEL

15 PLACES
TO SLEEP

---

5 pleasant
HOSTELS

431 **THE GENERATOR HOSTEL**

Smithfield Square
Smithfield &
Stoneybatter ⑥
+353 (0)1 901 0222
www.generatorhostels.com

Not so long ago, Dublin lacked a good range of inexpensive and safe hostels, but luckily they have started appearing. The Generator Hostel is one of the best: they offer good clean rooms, great design and a great bar, good prices, a friendly community in a prime location and some of the best burgers around.

432 **ISAACS HOSTEL**

2-5 Frenchman's Lane,
Mountjoy
O'Connell Street &
the Quays ④
+353 (0)1 855 6215
www.isaacs.ie

Mountjoy is a mixed bag when it comes to safety, and it's best to avoid walking home alone at night here. But the hostel you'll find here is certainly one of the best designed and maintained in Dublin, with an incredible wine-cellar-esque basement and a stunning brick façade dotted in flags and red paint. Facilities are basic but the prices for the rooms are very good.

433 BARNACLES HOSTEL

19 Temple Lane South
Temple Bar ③
+353 (0)1 671 6277
www.barnacles.ie

You may not get too much sleep at this hostel in the heart of Temple Bar, but if you're here to party, you're right in the middle of the action. (If you want peace and quiet, check out the other options listed.) There are a lot of services and facilities on offer here from free laundry and free walking tours to 24-hour security.

434 ASHFIELD HOSTEL

20 D'Olier St
Trinity College &
Old City ①
+353 (0)1 679 7734
www.ashfieldhostel.com

Well situated near the pubs and bars but not amongst them, so you can get away from the noise at night if you wish. As well as the usual dorm rooms (the prices of which are nothing special) there are basic private rooms, which can be quite pricy depending on the time of year. Lots of facilities and a free buffet breakfast.

435 ABIGAIL'S HOSTEL

7-9 Aston Quay
Temple Bar ③
+353 (0)1 677 9300
www.abigailshostel.com

A very central location, with the Liffey and O'Connell Street right there and Temple Bar back behind you; if you can shut out the noise at night, you couldn't be better off. The building is well laid out and very tidy and clean, with a lot of facilities and services. The rooms can be pricy and need to be booked way ahead in advance.

5

REASONABLY PRICED

lodgings

---

436 KING SITRIC

East Pier, Howth
North Dublin ⑧
+353 (0)1 832 5235
www.kingsitric.ie

An ocean view and the sound of gulls has got to count for something. If you book in advance as a couple you'll pay 150 euros a night for a standard room, and that's a very reasonable price for a hotel with beautiful rooms and a superb restaurant.

437 THE TRINITY CITY HOTEL

2 Pearse St
Trinity College &
Old City ①
+353 (0)1 648 1000
www.trinitycityhotel.com

Pearse Street is within walking distance of everything and everywhere, so this is a great hotel for those who like shopping or for those on a business trip. There are many different types of rooms (classic rooms, Georgian suites, ...) and they offer a number of special packages with price reductions. The food and the courtyard restaurant and garden are sublime.

438 NUMBER 31

31 Leeson Close
St Stephen's Green &
Grafton St ②
+353 (0)1 676 5011
www.number31.ie

At the gates to Dublin city centre lies this 'boutique guesthouse', housed in a Georgian townhouse. The rooms are homely and extremely comfortable, and the breakfast is supposedly the best in Ireland. The garden and courtyard are resplendent.

439 THE BELVEDERE HOTEL

Great Denmark St
North Dublin ④
+353 (0)1 873 7700
www.belvederehotel
dublin.com

A reliable and quite central three-star hotel, offering immaculate rooms and a great hotel bar. There are dinner and show packages, Irish traditional music nights and big screen TVs for watching sports. The staff are incredibly friendly and the rooms are spacious and modern with reasonable nightly rates.

440 THE SCHOOLHOUSE HOTEL

2-8 Northumberland
Road, Ballsbridge
South Dublin ⑨
+353 (0)1 667 5014
www.schoolhousehotel.com

A beautiful four-star red-bricked hotel with arched wooden beams on the inside, as well as comfy armchairs and a fire. There's a lovely area indoors and outdoors to enjoy a drink, and the food, prepared by head chef Francois Grelet, is excellent value. The prices here reflect the quality of the hotel as a whole.

438 **NUMBER 31**

5 hotels for sleeping
IN LUXURY

---

441 THE MARKER HOTEL

Grand Canal Square,
Docklands
O'Connell Street &
the Quays ④
+353 (0)1 687 5100
www.themarkerhotel
dublin.com

Strategically located beside the Bord Gais Energy Theatre is this five-star hotel. From floor to ceiling, inside and out, it is nothing short of impressive. Everything oozes style: the walls, the bar and, of course, the opulent rooms with Malin+Goetz products. The roof bar is the epitome of laid back cool.

442 THE MERRION HOTEL

Merrion Street Upper
St Stephen's Green &
Grafton St ②
+353 (0)1 603 0600
www.merrionhotel.com

This is the cream of the crop when it comes to style and extravagance. The swimming pool looks as if it is from an emperor's palace, there's a collection of fine art, and the rooms are fit for kings and queens. And there is the Restaurant Patrick Guilbaud, the only two-star Michelin restaurant in Ireland.

443 THE GIBSON HOTEL

Point Square
North Dublin ⑧
+353 (0)1 681 5000
www.thegibsonhotel.ie

A very cool, modern and uber-stylish four-star hotel, with corridors of glass and a lot of interesting modern art. The Gibson prides itself on offering you whatever you wish, whether that be quiet nights or music, drinks and dance.

444 THE SHELBOURNE HOTEL

27 St Stephen's Green
St Stephen's Green &
Grafton St ②
+353 (0)1 663 4500
www.marriott.com/hotels

The home away from home for the rich and famous. Enter past the top hat doormen, enjoy a fantastic White Russian at the bar and then think about what you'd like to do next: relax in your room or take on the fitness centre and indoor pool, or perhaps investigate the 24-hour dining options. Here, the world is your oyster.

445 THE FITZWILLIAM HOTEL

127-128 St Stephen's
Green
St Stephen's Green &
Grafton St ②
+353 (0)1 478 7000
www.fitzwilliamhotel
dublin.com

This nicely located and very chic five-star hotel takes you back to Georgian Dublin. Guests can ask for anything they want here, no whim is too big or too small. The bedrooms are huge and incredibly comfortable, the staff knowledgeable and friendly and there are two fine-dining restaurants.

441 THE MARKER HOTEL

HOWTH

20 ACTIVITIES
FOR WEEKENDS

5

OUTDOOR

adventures

---

446 WAKEDOCK WAKE PARK & PRO SHOP

South Dock Road, Grand
Canal Dock
South Dublin ⑨
+353 (0)1 664 3883
www.wakedock.ie

Wakeboarding is where you ride a shorter and fatter version of a surfboard while being towed by a motorboat. Fantastical aerial stunts and show-off manoeuvres are optional. It's a fun way to spend a few hours in the summer, and Dublin's Docklands provide a safe environment with a number of stunting obstacles.

447 GOLF

Various locations
www.gogolfing.ie

Ireland has a huge number and variety of golf courses; there are literally dozens and dozens of golf courses, to suit the beginner or the pro, in Dublin alone. Some of the best include Portmarnock (once home to The Walker Cup and The Irish Open) and the extraordinary Royal Dublin Golf Club located on North Bull Island.

448 SHELBOURNE RACES

AT: SHELBOURNE PARK
South Lotts Road
South Dublin ⑨
1890 269 969
www.igb.ie/shelbournepark

Shelbourne is famous for betting and dog racing, but has more to offer for a full night out. Casual drinks and dining overlooking the tracks, corporate functions and hen parties are all catered for. There is a free shuttle bus from Burgh Quay each Friday and Saturday night at 7 pm.

449 KITESURFING LESSONS

AT: PURE MAGIC

370 Clontarf Road,
Dollymount Beach
North Dublin ⑧
+353 (0)1 805 4912
www.puremagic.ie/dublin

Kitesurfing is a fusion of a few types of watersports, namely surfing, paragliding and windsurfing. You use the wind and a specially made power harness/kite to propel you forward on a board very similar to a wakeboard. Dollymount Strand is perfect for beginners as the water is very flat and shallow for a considerable distance out to sea.

450 RAFTING

AT: CANOE CENTRE

Mill Lane, Palmerstown
North Dublin ⑧
+353 (0)1 626 4363
www.rafting.ie

We admit this isn't white water rafting in the Grand Canyon but it's still incredible fun – and a lot safer. The adventure begins about 20 minutes away from the city centre in Palmerstown and ends on a section of the Liffey by Phoenix Park; the whole trip takes roughly 2,5 hours. Along the way there's natural beauty to enjoy and weirs to navigate.

446 DAVID O'CAOIMH AT WAKEDOCK WAKE PARK

5
DAY TRIPS
away from Dublin

---

451 GLENDALOUGH

Derrybawn, Glendalough
Co. Wicklow
www.glendalough.ie

This is well worth the one-hour drive south from the city centre (or around one hour and 20 minutes using St Kevin's Bus Services from St Stephen's Green). Glendalough, the 'valley of two lakes', is a stunning glacial valley in Co. Wicklow with spectacular surroundings, lots of monastic architecture and a museum and visitor centre.

452 BRÚ NA BÓINNE

Donore
Co. Meath
+353 (0)41 988 0300
*www.worldheritageireland.
ie/bru-na-boinne*

Most people will probably have heard of Newgrange (the 5000-year-old prehistoric monument and tomb) but the actual area is called Brú na Bóinne and contains not just Newgrange, but two other sites called Knowth and Dowth. Between them, Knowth in particular, the scale of megalithic art is staggering and it's one of the largest collections in Europe.

453 POWERSCOURT GARDENS AND WATERFALL

Powerscourt Estate,
Enniskerry
Co. Wicklow
+353 (0)1 204 6000
www.powerscourt.com

These are two different parts of one huge estate (each charges its own entrance fee). The Gardens stretch over 47 acres with a number of forests, walks, water features and various types of gardens (Japanese, Rose, Walled). The Waterfall is located 6 kilometres on from the estate comprised of hiking trails, picnic areas, a kiosk, parklands and a waterfall.

454 VICTOR'S WAY

Old Enniskerry Road,
Roundwood
Co. Wicklow
+353 (0)1 281 8505
www.victorsway.eu

It's unlikely you'll have seen anything like this before. Between 15th April and 15th September, this private park is open for visitors who love nothing better than a relaxing stroll… amidst huge statues of Hindu deities like Shiva, Ganesh, The Ferryman and many more. Read the online information before arrival.

455 TULACH A' TSOLAIS AND OULART HILL

Oulart
Co. Wexford
www.oularthill.ie

About a 3-hour round trip, this is a solid day away from it all, filled with history. There are many different walks, a number of holy stones, a fire-lit storytelling house, Fr. Murphy's Well, a church, remnants of the Battle of the Rising of Oulart Hill and the Tulach a' tSolais itself: a stunning piece of artwork opened in 1999 in dedication to this Rising.

5 unique
WALKS

456 DODDER WALK

Starts at Clonskeagh via
Milltown to Rathfarn-
ham shopping centre
South Dublin ⑨
www.walkingroutes.ie/
1161-Dodder-Trail.html

Clonskeagh is a nice part of Dublin to start off a walk. This is a fairly unchallenging walk, more or less in a straight line. It's almost 5 kilometres and follows alongside the River Dodder, bypassing two parks (Darty and Bushy), which makes it almost impossible to get lost.

457 HOWTH CLIFF PATH

22 Balscadden Road
Howth
North Dublin ⑧
www.irishtrails.ie/trail/
Howth---Cliff-Path-loop/107

This coastal trail of about 6 kilometres is a National Loop Walk. It starts at the DART station in Howth village and goes right out to the Nose of Howth, along the cliffs and then back inside past two golf courses. It's a very rugged and windy walk but the views and the sea air are amazing.

458 TICKNOCK FAIRY CASTLE LOOP

Dublin mountains
South Dublin ⑨
www.dublinmountains.ie/
recreation_sites/ticknock

Read the website link carefully to find the correct starting and ending point high in the Dublin mountains. The route is about 5.5 kilometres and takes in Fairy Castle (nothing but a mound of rocks really), Two Rock and Three Rock (which are really just exaggerated hills). The views and the cold fresh mountain air are like nothing else.

459 DONABATE TO PORTRANE LOOP TRAIL WALK

Fingal
North Dublin ⑧
www.walkingroutes.ie/
1866-Donabate-to-
Portrane-Loop.html

This loop-walk is longer than the others coming in at just over 12 kilometres and it covers some great ground. The views are spectacular, looking right out at Lambay Island at around the halfway point. The walk takes in the cliffs and the beaches below and circles two golf courses.

460 CARRICKGOLLOGAN FOREST WALK
(LEAD MINES WAY)

Near Shankill
Co. Dublin
South Dublin ⑨
www.coillteoutdoors.ie/
*index.php?id=173&rec_*
site=15&trail=20

This is a short looping walk of about 2 kilometres with the Carrickgollogan Forest at its centre. It's only a 30-metre climb but at it's highest point it's enough to see the Sugar Loaf mountain south and from west back around to east you can see Greystones, Bray and Killiney. A slight detour and you can find the Lead Mines Chimney. Be sure to read the website carefully.

457 HOWTH CLIFF PATH

5 stadiums for
SPORT FANS

———————

461 **THE AVIVA**
Lansdowne Road
South Dublin ⑨
+353 (0)1 238 2300
www.avivastadium.ie

This grand sporting stadium is the pride of the nation. The unique bowl-shaped arena was developed by Scott Tallon Walker architects and opened in 2010. It has a capacity for just over 57.000. It is the home of the Irish international rugby and football teams and also occasionally hosts American football and concerts.

462 **PARNELL PARK**
Donnycarney
North Dublin ⑧
+353 (0)1 831 2099
www.dublingaa.ie

Parnell Park is the home of Dublin GAA hurling, football and camogie with a capacity for 13,500. The All-Ireland Senior hurling championship, the All-Ireland Senior football championship, the Railway Cup and the Dublin county championships are all played here every year.

463 **RDS ARENA**
Merrion Road,
Ballsbridge
South Dublin ⑨
+353 (0)1 269 3224
www.leinsterrugby.ie

The RDS is a multi-purpose venue just as well known for the Dublin horse show and Ireland Comic Con as it is for Leinster rugby and Bruce Springsteen concerts (he has played here 11 times). The RDS has been hosting Rugby Union games since 2005 and became the official home of Leinster in 2007.

464 CROKE PARK

Jones' Road,
Drumcondra
North Dublin ⑧
+353 (0)1 819 2300
www.crokepark.ie/home

This is Europe's third biggest stadium, with a capacity of over 82.000 people. It's the home of the Gaelic Athletic Association and has existed in one form or another since 1880. It was the scene of the infamous 1920 Bloody Sunday massacre. The two biggest draws here are the GAA All-Ireland football and hurling championship finals.

465 DALYMOUNT PARK

Phibsborough
North Dublin ⑧
+353 (0)1 868 0923
www.bohemianfc.com

Opened in 1901 this stadium is now home to the League of Ireland football team Bohemian F.C., with a capacity of just over 4000. As of 2017 it is being shared with north Dublin rivals Shelbourne F.C. In the meantime Dalymount itself is undergoing an impressive redevelopment. Hopes are it will be finished by 2020 with a capacity of 10.000.

461 THE AVIVA

GHOST SIGNS

35 RANDOM FACTS AND URBAN DETAILS

5

UNUSUAL SIGHTS

to look out for

---

466 FATHER PAT NOISE PLAQUE

O'Connell Bridge
O'Connell Street &
the Quays ④

He sounds like a character from Father Ted ... or is this plaque dedicated to a real priest? It's neither. Father Pat Noise is a completely fictitious character and this is a hoax plaque installed by two mischievous brothers. So much effort. It was actually removed by the city council, but then reinstalled.

467 DODDER RHINO

Near the Dropping Well
bar in Milltown
South Dublin ⑨

Not a real rhino but a life size bronze statue of one, in the river Dodder just below Classon's Bridge behind the Dropping Well bar. Apparently it appeared overnight in 2002 and no one is willing to take responsibility for it. It does make for a nice photo for those lucky enough to stumble across it.

468 GIANT RED SQUIRREL ON THE SIDEWALL OF THE WORKSHOP GASTROPUB

10 Georges Quay
O'Connell Street &
the Quays ④

A giant red squirrel with a difference. This one is made entirely from rubbish by the environmental artist Artur Bordalo. Looming almost three stories high, it's an ingenious piece of artwork hoping to bring attention to the demise of our national animal under threat from both the grey squirrel and deforestation.

469 GULLIVER'S TRAVELS FRAMES

Another huge claim to fame for Dublin: Jonathan Swift is ours, and so is *Gulliver's Travels*. This most famous of stories is immortalised in the city with a series of pictorial frames. There are eight in total, individually set in a circular frame of brown terracotta brick with each depicting a scene from part 1 of the book.

470 RORY GALLAGHER'S GUITAR

Even Jimi Hendrix was in awe of blues musician Rory Gallagher. He gave everything he had when playing, so much so that rumour has it he actually sweated off the paint job on one of his first guitars. This commemorative Fender is in pretty good nick though. If you don't know his stuff, check out the songs Crest of a Wave and A Million Miles Away. Stunning.

470 RORY GALLAGHER'S GUITAR

5 historical
ODDITIES

471 KING GEORGE IV FOOTPRINTS

16 West Pier, Howth
North Dublin ⑨

This extravagant king, once the ruler of the UK and Ireland, bears his mark in the cement of Howth pier. In 1821 he arrived here for his 59th birthday in merry spirits (in other words: completely drunk); he was greeted amicably by the locals and his arrival was, well, literally cemented. In case you missed it, don't worry, his feet were very small.

472 NAPOLEON'S TOOTHBRUSH

AT: RCPI HERITAGE CENTRE,
SETANTA HOUSE

1 Setanta Place
St Stephen's Green &
Grafton St ②
+353 (0)1 863 9700
www.rcpi.ie/heritage-centre

Irish born Barry Edward O'Meara found himself selected as Napoleon's private physician while he was imprisoned in St. Helena. As thanks for his friendship Napoleon gave him one of his remaining possessions. You guessed it. His toothbrush.

473 THE FIGURE OF COURAGE - BULLET HOLES

O'Connell St
O'Connell Street &
the Quays ④

The Daniel O'Connell statue commemorates the Irish political leader who campaigned for Catholic emancipation and attempted to break the Act of Union. Despite his opposition to violence, during the 1916 Easter Rising his statue was peppered with bullets. And so was the winged Figure of Courage beneath him with one glaring bullet hole in her breast.

474 CAMINO STARTING POINT

St James's Gate
Kilmainham &
Liberties ⑤
+353 (0)85 781 9088
www.caminosociety.ie

Known by many names, the Camino de Santiago is a pilgrimage that follows a number of routes all leading to the Cathedral of Santiago de Compostela in Galicia northwest Spain. One such route begins at Dublin's own St James's Church, which will also issue your Irish Pilgrims Passport. Look for the blue and yellow St James's scallop shell, which is a symbol of the route.

475 ROBERT EMMET'S EXECUTION BLOCK

AT: PEARSE MUSEUM,
ST ENDA'S PARK
Grange Road,
Rathfarnham
South Dublin ⑧
+353 (0)1 493 4208
www.heritageireland.ie/
en/dublin/pearsemuseum-
stendaspark

Emmet was the leader of the failed rebellion of 1803 and as a result he was hanged and beheaded outside St Catherine's Church. Patrick Pearse, himself a leader of the 1916 Easter Rising, was fascinated with Emmet and he acquired the exact block Emmet was beheaded on. It has therefore been retained in the Pearse Museum.

5 intriguing
GHOST SIGNS

476 THE SICK AND INDIGENT ROOMKEEPERS SOCIETY

2 Palace St
St Stephen's Green &
Grafton St ②

Nowadays this society works as Dublin's oldest charity from its address on Leeson Street. But this address on Palace Street – the shortest street in Dublin – was its original location. They have left behind one of the best ghost signs here, with its unusual and original lettering over the full façade of the building.

477 READS CUTLERS

4 Parliament St
Temple Bar ③
www.readscutlers.com

This address has a lot of historical significance as Dublin's oldest shop. When it was established in 1670, it sold silverware, swords and instruments. Outside the signage is still there, inside is a perfectly preserved building that is now protected by the city council. You can't visit it, but the website is fascinating.

478 SWITZERS & CO

Above Brown Thomas
Grafton St
St Stephen's Green &
Grafton St ②

Above Brown Thomas on the Wicklow Street side of the building, is a small green and gold plaque saying 'Switzers & Co. Ltd'. Just before Brown Thomas bought Switzers in 1990, Switzers itself had been a successful luxury store expanding its original size by amalgamating six smaller shops into one large one.

479 THE COMBRIDGE GALLERIES & LITTLE MIDSHIPMAN

Above the Bailey pub
Duke St
St Stephen's Green &
Grafton St ②

On a ledge above the famous watering hole Bailey pub there is a sign that reads 'The Combridge Galleries' and below it there is a decorative midshipman (a rank of officer in the Royal Navy). The Combridge Galleries was in fact a business selling books and fine art. Founded in 1836, it closed shop by 2012, crippled by the recession.

480 FINN'S HOTEL

Leinster St South
Trinity College &
Old City ①

Follow the Trinity railings down Nassau Street away from Grafton Street and keep looking up until you can see this sign – each letter is eight bricks high. The hotel was run by a Tipperary couple and this is where Nora Barnacle, the future Mrs. James Joyce and his muse, was working when they first met in 1904.

5

SONGS *about* DUBLIN

481 DUBLIN IN THE RARE OULD TIMES
THE DUBLINERS

Written by composer and producer Pete St John, this typical old Irish ballad has become one of his best known songs about Dublin. It's a song of regret and loss and harking back to those younger, better days. It featured on The Dubliners album *Together Again* (1979).

482 ON RAGLAN ROAD
LUKE KELLY

This beautiful ballad was written by poet Patrick Kavanagh and put to music by Luke Kelly, a founding member of The Dubliners. Kelly used the music from the traditional number *The Dawning of the Day* alongside Kavanagh's words and the result was *On Raglan Road*, a stunning achievement.

483 BAD
U2

Before Michael Jackson got *Bad* on us in 1987, U2 were there first in 1984 with this classic number. Bono wrote the lyrics of this uneasy song about heroin addiction in the 1980's inner city Dublin. It is still to this day a staple of their live performances.

484 RAT TRAP
BOOMTOWN RATS

The Boomtown Rats never were a very cool band, unlike others on this list, but this is a catchy song with a great bassline and sax solo, and it's about being stuck in a depressing city – we can only guess they meant Dublin. Produced by Mutt Lange, it was released in 1978 and went straight to number one in the UK.

485 OLD TOWN
PHIL LYNOTT

This was the lead single of Lynott's second solo album he released in 1982 after he broke away from Thin Lizzy, Ireland's greatest hard rock band of all time. The song is about the breakup of a couple. The video was recorded all around Dublin city centre and features a number of obvious landmarks including the Ha'penny Bridge.

5 Dublin
B O O K S
to read

486 DUBLINERS
JAMES JOYCE

Enough about *Ulysses* (1922) and *A Portrait of the Artist as a Young Man* (1916), for me *Dubliners* (1914), Joyce's short story collection, is his masterpiece. Focusing on the Irish middle class in and around Dublin, there are 15 stories of friendship, love, regret, heartbreak, comedy and religion. The final heart-wrenching story *The Dead* is often considered the best of the bunch; it was adapted into an Oscar-nominated film in 1987.

487 AT SWIM-TWO-BIRDS
FLANN O'BRIEN

This book, published in 1939, has long been considered Flann O'Brien's (real name: Brian O'Nolan) masterpiece. It's a very Irish story that deals with the small day-to-day stuff while also using a stream of consciousness-type narrative, later in the novel, to pull the story in all directions. While challenging at times, it is also very rewarding.

488 THE GINGER MAN
JAMES PATRICK DONLEAVY

The Ginger Man by the Irish-American writer J.P. Donleavy was initially published in Paris in 1955, but it was subsequently banned in Ireland on grounds of obscenity. Set in 1940's Dublin it tells the story of Sebastian Dangerfield and his outlandish antics. It would go on to sell 45 millions copies and has never gone out of print.

489 MELMOTH THE WANDERER
CHARLES MATURIN

Maturin wrote a number of successful Gothic novels and plays and could count Victor Hugo and Alexandre Dumas among his admirers. *Melmoth the Wanderer* (1820), his masterpiece, revolves around a young Dublin student called John Melmoth who, after selling his soul to the devil in exchange for an extra 150 years of life, is tasked with passing on the pact.

490 STRUMPET CITY
JAMES PLUNKETT

This historical novel from 1969 is set in the years leading up to and following the Dublin lock-out (1913). It's a sweeping epic that covers the lives of about a dozen characters and jumps forward and back between 1907 and 1914. It's about how the city shaped the characters and how in turn the characters shape the city around them. A classic.

5 Dublin
FILMS
to see

---

491 THE SNAPPER
1933

The Snapper was shot in Dublin and revolves around young pregnant Sharon who refuses to tell anyone who the father of the baby is. The film is based on the hilarious book by Booker prize-winning author Roddy Doyle. Another two of his novels, featuring some of the same characters, were also adapted to screen: *The Commitments* and *The Van*.

492 ADAM & PAUL
2004

Adam and Paul could be any of the heroin addicts in Dublin (emblematic of a scourge this city is struggling to contain). They aren't really very likeable but they certainly give a voice to a demographic that rarely finds one. In some small way, you can't help feeling sorry for their tireless desperation in this odd and tragic buddy movie.

493 INTERMISSION
2003

This comedy/crime film is probably best remembered for two things; one – Colin Farrell's memorable role as the manic Lehiff on the run from the equally manic copper Jerry Lynch (a brilliant Colm Meaney) and two – the habit of putting brown sauce in your tea.

494 MY LEFT FOOT
1989

This film was Sheridan's debut feature and the first one of three incredibly important and influential Irish films (the others being *The Field* and *In the Name of the Father*). It was a massive stepping stone in his career and that of actor Daniel Day-Lewis, who received world renown for his Oscar-winning portrayal of artist Christy Brown, who suffered from cerebral palsy.

495 GLASSLAND
2014

This Irish drama, directed by Gerard Barrett, follows young broke taxi driver John (Jack Reynor) as he tries to balance out taking care of his alcoholic mother (Toni Collette) and spending time with his younger Down syndrome brother. It's gritty stuff all right, but timely and realistic and superbly acted – it makes for a rewarding viewing.

5 important
TIPS FOR TRAVELLERS

<hr>

496 **AIRCOACH**
www.aircoach.ie

There's really no other way to get back and forth from the airport than the Aircoach. It's not that expensive and Dublin is a small enough city so you'll get where you need to go in no time. There should be an Aircoach kiosk and terminal right outside the airport doors. Check the website carefully for times.

497 **TIPPING & PRICES**

Tipping in restaurants is standard. Tips should be around 12%, but most people just calculate 10% and throw a little on top. Always check your receipt first to make sure it wasn't already included. Tipping taxi drivers is not that common anymore and it isn't expected. As for prices; if you want to stay away from expensive shopping, avoid Grafton Street and if you want to avoid expensive drinking, skip Temple Bar.

498 LEAP CARD

If you've ever visited or lived in London, then you'll know of the Oyster card. This one is the same deal: buy the card, top it up at any DART (train) station or newsagent's and then use it for all DARTs, Dublin buses and Luas (tram). Make sure this is one of the first things you buy; without this card travelling around Dublin is very expensive.

499 DISCOUNTS

Almost all the attractions and services in Dublin have some form of discounts for the elderly, for those on benefits and for students, national or foreign. As long as you have the relevant photo ID, you should be fine. Oh, while we're on the topic, it is wise to take your photo ID with you on nights out. Some bars/clubs are very strict after midnight on weekends; while most venues are over 18s/21s, others, if they wish can enforce an over 26s or even 28s policy late at night.

500 WI-FI

www.wifispc.com

There are the obvious coffee shop choices like Starbucks where you can stay as long as you want to, at least if you purchase something. But there are also others where you can sit and avail of unprotected free access, but where? Someone put it all together on this website/map. There's also a link on the site that allows you to download their app to your phone.

Leabharlanna Poiblí Chathair Baile Átha Cliath

Dublin City Public Libraries

INDEX

COLOPHON

EDITING AND COMPOSING – Shane O'Reilly

GRAPHIC DESIGN – Joke Gossé and Tinne Luyten

PHOTOGRAPHY – Sam Mellish – www.sammellish.com

COVER IMAGE – The Bernard Shaw, Richmond St

The addresses in this book have been selected after thorough independent research by the author, in collaboration with Luster Publishers. The selection is solely based on personal evaluation of the business by the author. Nothing in this book was published in exchange for payment or benefits of any kind.

D/2017/12.005/5
ISBN 978 94 6058 2028
NUR 506

© 2017, Luster, Antwerp

www.lusterweb.com – www.the500hiddensecrets.com
info@lusterweb.com

Printed in Italy by Printer Trento.

MIX
Paper from responsible sources
FSC® C015829